Magic from the Soul of Nature

When I sit in my springtime garden and see last year's autumn oak leaves woven among grasses and bright blooming daffodils, or when the sky is dark with winter rain and all of the power of the elements is unleashed, or bees and butterflies busy themselves around me in the summer warmth, then I am moved and shaken, filled with love and awe and reverence. For ours is a religion of the earth, and our most powerful encounters with the divine are often in the little things that pass by those whose lives are entangled with the cut and thrust of modern life.

—ELEN HAWKE

Empower your encounters with the divine and enhance your magical practice. Craft Elder Elen Hawke presents step-by-step instructions on the chakras, seasonal rites, magic, spells, meditation, and divination. This poetic, positive, and life-affirming guide will take you to the next level of Craft skill and knowledge.

About the Author

Elen Hawke is a British witch who lives in Oxford, England, with her husband and a house full of animals. She has a grown daughter and son. Elen is a photographer, illustrator, and has been a professional astrologer for twenty-nine years and a tarot reader for twelve. These days, she divides her time between healing, teaching witchcraft, meditation, and chakra work, and celebrating the moons and festivals with the rest of the coven to which she belongs.

To Write to the Author

If you wish to contact the author or would like more information about this book, please write to the author in care of Llewellyn Worldwide and we will forward your request. Both the author and publisher appreciate hearing from you and learning of your enjoyment of this book and how it has helped you. Llewellyn Worldwide cannot guarantee that every letter written to the author can be answered, but all will be forwarded. Please write to:

Elen Hawke
℅ Llewellyn Worldwide
P.O. Box 64383, Dept. 0-7387-0172-6
St. Paul, MN 55164-0383, U.S.A.

Please enclose a self-addressed stamped envelope for reply,
or $1.00 to cover costs. If outside U.S.A., enclose
international postal reply coupon.

Many of Llewellyn's authors have websites with additional information and resources. For more information, please visit our website at http://www.llewellyn.com

THE SACRED ROUND

A WITCH'S GUIDE TO MAGICAL PRACTICE

ELEN HAWKE

2002
Llewellyn Publications
St. Paul, Minnesota 55164-0383, U.S.A.

FIRST EDITION
First Printing, 2002

Book design and editing by Karin Simoneau
Cover design by Gavin Duffy
Interior art by Kerigwen Hunter

Library of Congress Cataloging-in-Publication Data
Pending

Llewellyn Worldwide does not participate in, endorse, or have any authority or responsibility concerning private business transactions between our authors and the public.

All mail addressed to the author is forwarded but the publisher cannot, unless specifically instructed by the author, give out an address or phone number.

Llewellyn Publications
A Division of Llewellyn Worldwide, Ltd.
P.O. Box 64383, Dept. 0-7387-0172-6
St. Paul, MN 55164-0383, U.S.A.
www.llewellyn.com

 Printed in the United States of America on recycled paper

For Stephen

Contents

Acknowledgments

Heartfelt thanks to the following people: my daughter and husband for believing in me; Kate and Lin for encouraging me; my editor Karin Simoneau for doing such a superb job (I always wondered why authors thanked their editors, and now I know . . . Karin, you're the best!); Kerigwen for her sensitive and beautiful illustrations, which match the text so well; Nancy Mostad for being supportive; and lastly, Kala Trobe, for the gift of an unexpected friendship and the novel experience of exchanging ideas with another writer.

Introduction

There are many books on witchcraft, Wicca, and paganism, but not all of them go beyond basic circle casting, magic, and ritual. This is fine when you first start to practice, but eventually the time comes when you want to explore further, delve deeper, and develop your skills. Of course, you can acquire this knowledge through experimentation and trial and error, but how can you be sure you are "doing it right"? What if you make mistakes? And how about the little methods and snippets of knowledge that could put the pieces of the puzzle together for you? The answers are usually quite simple, but you don't always discover that by yourself. Some people are lucky enough to have a teacher or training group on which to rely when they want to expand their knowledge and experience. However, many individuals and groups have started out of their own volition, and, therefore, have only books to turn to when they want to learn more.

This book is intended as a companion volume to my book *In The Circle*, so the techniques learned there can be built upon and expanded. I hope it will fill the gap for people, explain where to go next, and how to learn more about magic and ritual, the festivals, the moon's phases, the elements, chakra work, meditation, and all the other ingredients that make up the practice of modern witchcraft. However, it covers a certain amount of basic information as well, so it could be used by someone new to the Craft.

The book contains exercises and rituals, meditations and spells. It can be read methodically from end to end, or dipped into as needed. Although the chapters follow each other in a definite sequence, each section is informative in its own right. It is up to individual readers to determine how much work they want to put into the exercises, though the skills of the Craft do require a certain amount of effort to master. I hope the process will be an enjoyable one.

CHAPTER ONE

Witches and the Craft

Witchcraft is a joyous celebration: of nature; of the seasons; of earth, fire, air, water, and spirit; of the waxing and waning moon and the fiery sun; of the life force manifesting as the Goddess and God. It is a form of spirituality that honours the environment and the other species with which we share our world, and which seeks to respect the rights of others. This is not a path that is trodden by a chosen few, or within only a handful of countries, or by people of a particular culture or skin colour, age, or gender. Witchcraft is universal, though its modern practitioners are far fewer in number than those of the major world religions.

In ancient times a witch was a shaman, probably a medicine man or woman; in classical times he would have been a clairvoyant or soothsayer, possibly working in one of the famous oracle sites such as Delphi; in medieval times a witch was often the village wise woman or cunning man, the purveyor of curses, fertility spells, abortions, healing charms and herbs, something of an expert in weather lore. There were and are witches among the indigenous peoples of many countries. In modern times, witches have a little, or a lot, of all their ancestors' abilities (though few of us now would think it either acceptable or ethical to manipulate another or harm life), but in addition, many have developed skills such as astrology, the reading of cards, and other forms of divination, along with a flair for creating ritual and a keen insight into the psychological workings of the human mind.

Unlike some of the witches of old, their modern counterparts are bound by an incredibly strict code of ethics, something partly bequeathed to us by ritual magicians and the occult societies of the late nineteenth and early twentieth centuries. It is no longer acceptable for pagans of any persuasion to do harm to another in any way whatsoever, or to use occult means to take what is not theirs. Also, with the environmental crisis we face today worldwide, witches have a deep and keenly developed concern for the land and the creatures that live on it, and they can often be found involved in conservation groups and protest movements.

There is often no way to tell a witch from a nonwitch, unless they are comfortable with dressing up to the role. Witches are usually ordinary people, drawn from all walks of life, whose spirituality just happens to be pagan. And when I say from all walks of life, I mean just that: I have known witches who are shop assistants, lawyers, computer programmers, psychologists, bank clerks, nurses, doctors, and teachers, among many other professions.

Some people are open about their religious views and some are not. We still live in an atmosphere that is less tolerant than we might wish, and in some areas—for instance, rural backwaters in Britain and the Deep South in America—to announce one's pagan leanings would expose one to the risk of abuse ranging from insults and foul language to actual harm to one's self or family or property. Much of this prejudice has come about because of negative stereotypes created or perpetuated by the media, film, and novels, and by suppression and misunderstanding at the hands of other religions. However, the general public is becoming better informed and more enlightened, and many of us now enjoy a climate of greater religious tolerance and freedom than this, and live openly and amicably with those of other spiritual persuasions.

To practice witchcraft, you don't need to go to a special building on a set day of the week, although certain days and points in the year are sacred to us. It's possible to be a witch simply by observing the seasons, gardening in accordance with certain moon's phases, or lighting a daily candle to honour the deities.

The way witches perceive deity is also somewhat different from the way mainstream religions perceive it. Some witches honour only the Goddess, though they may see her through the faces and guises of many different cultures and historical times. Others revere the God as well. To some, divinity is one being, though it shows a masculine and feminine side. To others, there are two distinct deities, one male and one female. To others still, there is a multitude of gods and goddesses, while to yet others, the Goddess and God show many aspects that are seen as the separate deities of cultural pantheons such as the Greek, Roman, Egyptian, Hindu, Norse, and Celtic.

The Goddess and God are everywhere: not in some special place like the ritual circle, or hovering around our altars and shrines, but in every part of our lives. When I sit in my springtime garden and see last autumn's oak leaves woven among grasses and bright blooming daffodils, or when the sky is dark with winter rain and all the power of the elements is unleashed, or bees and butterflies busy themselves around me in the summer warmth, then I am moved and shaken, filled with love and awe and reverence. For ours is a religion of the earth, and our most powerful confrontations with the divine are often in the little things that pass by those whose lives are entangled with the cut and thrust of modern life.

The Goddess and the God live within each of us, and we live within them. The divine is part of the world . . . *is* the world. Nothing exists that is not a part of the thrilling and sacred dance of life. But many among us feel that the wonder of life did not come into being because of a finite act of creation, as is taught by the monotheistic religions such as Judaism, Christianity, and Islam: we believe that creation never stops, that everything goes on evolving; life goes on discovering itself. Part of our contribution to this ongoing formation is to realise ourselves and our own creativity, to become fully realised beings while retaining our sense of interconnectedness with everything else with which we share this universe. Within paganism, we express and experience these ideas through following the cycles of the moon and the seasons, paying special attention to certain significant points on these interlocking rounds.

Divinity is a concept that humans have developed to help us understand the part of spirituality that will not fit into words, or even into ideas that can be fully formulated and rounded out. We clothe the numinous in symbols and forms taken from the world we can see and hear, touch and taste, for we cannot give shape to it in any other way. Because we are creatures of matter, we best understand a reality that appears solid to us. Our minds may be able to conceptualise more abstract hypotheses, but our hearts relate best to something we feel we can recognise with our senses.

Witches and pagans generally understand this need to conceptualise our spirituality, and we weave symbols into ritual. Even those of us who don't work within a sacred circle still perform small rituals such as lighting a candle before a representation of the Goddess or God, or decorating our

homes with seasonal flowers, fruits, and greenery. We may
come together in groups to celebrate moon rites, especially
at the full moon, or to rejoice as one of the eight ancient festivals arrives.

Because pagans no longer have very many temples or
other permanent sacred structures, many of us create our
own sacred space, a temporary environment existing on
other levels as well as the earthly, an environment that we
dismantle again once our rite is over. Such a psychic temple
is constructed with etheric or astral energy by our minds,
and is invisible to ordinary eyesight, though it can be seen
with our deeper senses. Within our sacred space we practice
rituals of celebration, meditation, and magic.

Some witches are content to practice their craft in nonritualistic ways, planting seeds, baking bread, raising children, doing whatever work they do as an offering to the
Goddess and God, celebrating the major turning points of
the year with food and drink and song, but never delving
deeper into occult lore. These are good ways to follow the
path of the spirit, and we can all benefit from holding them
close to our hearts. But for some of us, these things are not
enough on their own; we want to dedicate more time and
effort to our spirituality, to evolve a celebratory and spiritual
life built on profound magical and ritual practice.

The purpose of this book is to provide the tools needed to
build such a practice, or to extend any ritual framework
already in use. These building blocks include the elements,
meditation, chakra work, ways to raise and shape energy,
and magic. All these skills can be treated fairly superficially,
and they will still develop in time. But choosing to work
hard, studying, practicing, and trying different things will
bring greater rewards, along with fulfillment and a keen
awareness of the spiritual truths behind it all.

CHAPTER TWO

Ritual and Sacred Space

Some people follow the Craft very simply, lighting a candle daily to honour the Goddess and God and to ask for peace and clarity in their lives, or communing with deity when they are in the garden or out in the countryside. Others may have a permanent altar or shrine at which they celebrate the seasonal festivals and the full moons, and this may contain their magical tools, images of deities, flowers, shells, stones, and other objects considered sacred to them, or maybe a tarot card or other picture that represents qualities on which they are working at present, and possibly cords, candles, or other objects that are part of an ongoing spell. Some witches do all of these things, and also create temporary consecrated space when they want to practice ritual, either alone or with others.

Even if you want to do complex rituals, and most of your spiritual work is done this way, it is still a good idea to have a permanent place in your home where you can go to meditate, or just to have quiet time alone. Many of the exercises in this book suggest that you sit in such a space, before an altar or shrine. For some people, their space will contain familiar and well-loved objects, to others the setup will change with the seasons or the moon's cycle, or may reflect a phase they are going through, or reminders of spiritual or emotional strengths they wish to acquire. The point is that all of us need a place where we can be at peace, where we know we won't be disturbed; a space where our own energies will gradually permeate, making it feel familiar, comfortable, and safe. This place need not be large or elaborate (a corner of your bedroom will do), as long as it is the way you want it to be. In addition, lighting candles or burning incense will help you to relax and enter the frame of mind necessary for spiritual study. Eventually you will find that just settling into your space will prepare you for magical or meditative work, in the same way that putting on special clothes or jewelry (or removing clothes and going skyclad) prepares you for ritual.

You may find you are content to do all your magical work in your personal space, without ever going to the trouble of casting a full circle, or maybe just drawing a circle of protection around you with your mind. However, a fully fledged magical circle has the advantage of acting like a container, conserving and amplifying energies until you are ready to use them; it is also a safe place, somewhere between the world of everyday life and the spiritual realms, an extension of your own mystical centre and that of everyone else with you. It keeps out noise, distractions, and stray energies; it also balances you because it focuses the elements of earth, air, fire, water, and ether within and around you. It is, in fact, a temple on both the material and astral planes, and it remains in place until you choose to disperse it.

Within the circle, magic, dance, song, reverence, and celebration can take place, along with meditation, divination, healing, and poetry. Here the eight seasonal festivals are observed, as well as lunar rites, and we can meet the Goddess and God, share food and drink, and draw close to each other.

The following sections describe the magical tools needed within the circle, and the elements with which they are associated. It goes on to give a basic pattern for circle casting and ritual. This is intended as recap, as the purpose of this book is to give suggestions and exercises for those wishing to deepen their practice and lay a firmer foundation. However, there should be enough information here for people who are new to witchcraft and have never cast a circle or used magic before.

Magical Tools

Some people have a full set of magical equipment; others get away with a minimum of utensils. We are all different, and how you work is up to you. If you enter one of the Wiccan traditions, such as the Alexandrian or Gardnerian, you will be expected to make or buy the full set of equipment, and the working tools of the Craft will be presented to you as part of your initiation. Other traditions may be less bothered about having the correct tools. It's possible to work ritual without any sort of props at all, and indeed doing so is part of training for most witches. But most of us relate better to using the tools of the trade, so to speak, even if we are earthy kitchen witches who cast the circle with the vegetable knife and grab the nearest tea cup for the communion drink.

The Athame

This is the ritual knife used to project energy to form the magic circle, and sometimes to channel energy into a spell. Traditionally it should be made of steel and have a black

Magical Tools

wooden handle, but can be any colour and made entirely of
wood, silver, bronze, or stone, plus other variations. It is
ruled by air.

Athames can be bought ready-made from occult and new
age shops, or handmade. Alternatively, a kitchen or sheath
knife can be used, but the blade must be blunt to avoid accidents. Avoid secondhand knives, as they may have previ-
ously been put to dubious use.

The Wand

The wand is ruled by fire. It can be used instead of the
athame to cast the circle, but is more commonly used to
direct energy into spells. Wands are very easy to make, and
should be cut to a comfortable length—from elbow to fingertips or a bit longer is good. I prefer not to cut living
wood, and use fallen wood instead. If you insist on taking a
piece from a tree, ask the tree for permission first, and if
you intuitively feel you shouldn't cut it, then don't. Be
careful to select and cut in a way that won't badly damage
the tree, and leave something in exchange, such as a hair
from your head; this may sound silly, but it is good occult
practice; it gives something of yourself in exchange for
what the tree has given you, and it gives the reminder that
we should never take without being prepared to give back
in some way.

The Pentacle

Ruled by earth, the pentacle is a metal, wooden, or ceramic
disk about five or six inches across, on which is drawn or
inscribed a pentagram and possibly other symbols such as
those used in Wicca. Water and salt containers are placed
on it to be consecrated, and it can be used to "ground" spells
into reality by placing the spell ingredients on the pentacle.
Food can be placed on it to be blessed at the end of the rite.

You can make your own pentacle or buy one from occult suppliers.

The Censer

This is ruled by air and is used to burn incense during ritual. Any small fireproof dish or container can be used as a censer, though small brass ones are readily available from shops selling Indian crafts. Some people use a shell or terra cotta dish. Place the censer on a fireproof surface when lit, and be careful not to touch it with bare hands.

Loose incense is burned on charcoal blocks within the censer, though you could also use cone incense.

The Chalice

This is the container in which wine, juice, or water is passed round at the end of the rite. It is an object belonging to the element of water. Metal chalices are more hard-wearing, though glass, pottery, or china is okay. It's nice to stick with the old-fashioned goblet shape, but that's up to you. If you work within a group, then a large container may be needed.

The Cauldron

Not everyone has one of these, but they are very useful for holding candles or seasonal greenery during rituals, and for keeping spell candles safe. The cauldron, like the chalice, belongs to water. Large cast-iron ones can be purchased from antique shops, market stalls, and occult stores, but containers of a similar shape to the cauldron, though made of copper or other metals, can sometimes be bought from shops selling Far Eastern imports such as *kelims* and other rugs.

Bowls for Water and Salt

These should be small enough to fit on your altar with all the other tools.

Candles

Candles are placed, one in each of the four directions of east, south, west, and north, at the perimeter of the space where the circle will be cast, and represent the four basic elements. These can be in the elemental colours or in white, and they are referred to as point candles. Additionally, there should be two more candles on the altar—one for the Goddess and one for the God. Aside from this, candles of various colours can be used in spells. They can be bought almost anywhere, but they should be consecrated through the elements before use so that any residual energies from their manufacture and storage can be removed, leaving them clean and ready for your magical purpose.

There is a set of colour correspondences for candles in chapter 8, "Magical Practice."

Cords

Lengths of cords of various colours are sometimes used in spell work, and this is described in greater detail in chapter 8. The best type of cords are those used in upholstery, and these are available from haberdashery departments and stores that sell materials for dressmaking.

The Broom

This piece of equipment is optional. It is used to sweep the perimeter of the circle, not to remove dust and fluff but to cleanse away psychic debris. The sound of the broom is very relaxing, and many witches find it helps them to move into the tranquil frame of mind needed in ritual. Besoms, the old-fashioned witches brooms, are often sold in garden centres and hardware stores for sweeping up garden rubbish. If you like, you can tie coloured ribbons round the twig part.

The Altar

An altar can be permanently set up in the room where rituals take place, or it can be brought out when needed. It should be large enough to contain a set of working tools, plus food, ingredients for spells, flowers, and so on. Some people build a structure especially for the purpose, while others make use of a shelf or coffee table, which reverts to its usual function after the rite has ended.

The Book of Shadows

This is the personal magical diary kept by many witches. In it you write all your spells and rituals, meditations, dreams, and any other aspects of your spiritual practice. It can be a beautiful book with gold-blocked edges, or a loose-leaf file, or even a file on the hard drive of your computer.

Clothing and Jewelry

Some people work naked or skyclad, some wear special robes, and others come in their everyday dress. Whichever you do, remove your shoes indoors as a mark of respect. If you wear loose clothing, be careful around naked candle flames and, at the very least, have tight-fitting sleeves.

Many witches like to put on special jewelry during rituals: a pendant, bracelets, rings, or, for women, the traditional amber and jet priestess's necklace.

Sacred Space

We create sacred space so we can have somewhere outside of our everyday world, beyond clock time, in which to perform acts of magic and celebration. These activities could be undertaken anywhere, but working within an environment set apart helps us to slip into the frame of mind necessary to concentrate or to achieve deeper states of mind. The following section describes the way I set up and cast the circle and perform any work. Most traditions use a similar pattern, though they may do things in a slightly different order.

Cleansing Bath

This can be done either before or after setting up. The idea is to relax you, cleanse away any stress and emotional negativity, and put you in a frame of mind appropriate for the work to follow. A handful of sea salt and herbs can be very refreshing.

Setup

The circle itself can be as little as six feet (or even less) in diameter for a single person, and ten feet or more for a group. Use the whole room if you want.

If you want to use a broom, have one near. And if you want to raise energy, bring out a drum.

Place the cauldron in the centre of the circle or near the altar.

Put the point or directional candles in their appropriate compass directions. Use white candles for each, or yellow for east/air, red for south/fire, blue or blue-green for west/water, and green or brown for north/earth.

Put the altar either in the centre or the north of the space where you will cast your circle. On it, place your magical tools, including: the chalice of fluid for the "cakes and wine" at the end of the rite; the Goddess and God candle; flowers, fruit, or other decorations, including seasonal ones such as grain at Lammas or holly at Yule; food for the end of the rite; a bowl of water; a container of salt (preferably sea salt, as this is very pure and, consequently, works powerfully); the censer with a fresh charcoal block inside; incense appropriate for this particular rite; any ingredients to be used in spells, such as candles; a candle snuffer and candle holders.

Light the point candles and altar candles, and then light the charcoal, readying it for incense.

Sweep the perimeter of the circle with the broom if desired. This should be done slowly and rhythmically while visualising any psychic residue being swept away.

Grounding and Centring

The purpose of this is to release tension and get the energies flowing equally between the chakras, which will gently open during this process, ready for spiritual work. The chakras are described fully in chapter 4.

Stand upright with your feet slightly apart.

Relax, and begin to breathe slowly and deeply.

Let your breath reach deeper and deeper into your body until it begins to attain its own rhythm of inward and outward breath.

As you breathe out, begin to see any tension and anxiety leave you as a muddy gray stream flowing out through the nostrils.

As you breathe in, visualise energising life force flowing into your lungs as golden white light.

Continue until you feel relaxed but alert, then calmly sprinkle incense on the glowing charcoal in the censer.

Cleansing with the Elements

This is done with the purpose of removing any residual negativity that might interfere with the ritual, and both the area of the circle and its occupants are cleansed. It is done with a bowl of salted water to represent water and earth, and the censer of fiery charcoal and smoking incense to represent air and fire. Water is a widely accepted cleanser, but it absorbs negativity and so must first be cleansed and then primed with salt (a naturally clean substance in a psychic sense) so it doesn't pick up any more astral dirt.

Place the bowl of water on the pentacle upon your altar.

Hold the handle of your athame between the palms of your hand, lower the tip of the blade into the water, then visualise light flowing down your arms and out from the knife into the bowl, purifying the water. Say words similar to:

> **I cleanse and consecrate this water,**
> **that it may purify sacred space.**
> **By the power of Goddess and God.**

Put the salt bowl on the pentacle and put the athame tip in, watching the stream of light from it filling the bowl. Salt is already clean, but needs to be blessed so it is primed for its work of keeping the water pure, so use words such as:

> **I bless this salt that it might protect the sacred circle.**
> **By the power of Goddess and God.**

Now add three pinches of salt to the water and stir it gently.

Starting in the north, walk clockwise round the edge of the circle, sprinkling salted water as you go. Imagine that the water is cleansing the circle and beginning to seal its edge.

Finally, sprinkle salted water over yourself and anyone else present.

Sprinkle more incense on the charcoal, then carry the censer round, visualising it cleansing the perimeter of the circle and continuing the task of building a barrier of protection. Obviously, you can't carry the censer with bare hands, so it will need to be carried by a fireproof tray or container, or suspended by chains.

Waft the incense smoke over yourself and anyone else present.

Casting the Circle

The circle is formed with etheric energy, which is drawn into the body then projected out through an implement such as a wand or the blade of an athame, via one or more chakras. Imagine yourself drawing up energy similar to the life force you drew in while centring. Send the energy down the arm and hand and out through the blade in a focused stream of light. The colour this appears to you (either visually or in your mind's eye) will depend on which chakra is gathering and transmitting the power.

Beginning at the north and walking round clockwise, hold your athame or wand at arm's length in your dominant hand (the one you write with), and begin to project a steady stream of light out through the point.

Slowly walk round the circle, sending the beam of light out as you go so you form a barrier of light round the edge of the circle.

When you reach the eastern part of the circle, begin to say an invocation for circle casting, such as:

I call up thy power:
O Circle, be thou a boundary of protection between
the material world and the realm of the gods.

Of course, the gods are here in the world as well as in other realms of being, but you want to create a sense of an otherworldly place where you can set aside the concerns of daily living and contact the inner realms of the deeper mind.

Continue round the circle until you come back to the north, and the barrier of protection is sealed.

Calling in the Quarters

Focusing the elements is a necessary part of ritual. The elements are energies that exist throughout the whole of life (a

full exploration of them is described in the next chapter).
Concentrating on them in ritual makes sure any work done
in the circle is protected and balanced; it brings in necessary
powers that aid in magical work. If you don't summon the
quarters as part of circle casting, then you will feel off centre
and very strange. We depend on elemental factors throughout all aspects of our lives, whether emotional, mental, physical, or spiritual, and we can't function properly without
them, so it is extremely important to include them when
building a circle—which is, in a sense, a place apart from
the material world, into which we need to bring the worldly
powers.

Walk clockwise to the eastern quarter of the circle.

Facing the eastern point candle, visualise the qualities of air.

Visualise yellow light surrounding the eastern part of the circle, or draw a pentagram in the air before you with your
wand or athame. Start at top left, go diagonally to bottom
left, diagonally to centre right, straight across to centre
left, diagonally to bottom right, diagonally to top right to
join the top point, then back to bottom left. See this pentagram as glowing with yellow light.

Call up the powers of air by saying something like:

Powers of the east, powers of air,
I call you into the circle to empower our rite
and guard our sacred space.
Hail and welcome.

Go to the south and repeat the process, but visualising fire
qualities and a flaming red pentagram or red light.

Summon west and water with blue.

Summon earth and the north with brown or green.

The circle is now cast, taking you into a place between the levels of being, sacred space set apart from worldly activity.

Raising Energy

To work ritual successfully, you need to use etheric energy. If you rely on your own supply, you will become tired very quickly, so it is necessary to raise an extra supply by dancing, singing, chanting, or playing an instrument such as a drum. There are various songs and chants that witches use for this purpose, and which they sometimes repeat while dancing or running in a circle with linked hands. Once the power is raised, the circle will contain it like a reservoir, waiting for you to channel and shape it.

Invoking the Goddess and God

At this stage in the ritual, it is time to invite the presence of the deities. In the Craft, our deities are very approachable and can be called on by anyone, not just certain individuals; our gods do not dwell only in some lofty sphere detached from the world, but are present within ourselves and the rest of the universe of form. By invoking them, we call forth that part of our own being, and that of others with us, which is divine, though the Goddess and God appear to come into the circle from outside as well.

If you are doing a particular kind of magic, or are celebrating one of the festivals, you may want to invite the presence of a specific deity or deities; for example, Brighid at Imbolc, or Mercury if you want help with writing or some other form of communication. It pays to study the different gods and goddesses so you fully understand whom you are calling upon and how they are likely to relate to you or your magical aims. It isn't always a good idea to mix deities from different pantheons in the same ritual, as the energies may not blend very well. Of course, you may want to relate only

to the Goddess and God as abstracts, without personifying
them too much, or to the Lady and her horned Lord.

Various other chapters in the book give examples of invoking the deities, so I won't go into it in detail here. The main aim is to ask them to be present and to offer help and protection, to bless your work or help you draw close to them. Whatever your beliefs about the gods, you will sense the arrival of a presence when you invoke deity.

The Focus of the Rite

A ritual may be used for celebration alone, or for healing and magic, meditation or divination, as well as communing with the divine. If magic or healing are done, they make use of the reserves of energy that were produced earlier in the rite. I have described magic elsewhere, including how to focus power into a candle, cord, or other object as part of a spell. However, working with a cone of power is slightly different, and I will explain that in detail later in this chapter, along with other methods of shaping and directing power.

Etheric energy is highly malleable and can be shaped with the mind. It is used to charge spells, intent, visualisation, and so on. Shaping the power can be done by feel alone, or by seeing it as bright, crackling, or flowing light or energy. When you want to use it, start feeling or seeing yourself drawing this energy up, gathering it in through your aura. If you want to direct it into an object, such as a bowl of seeds, gather it, then project it in an intense stream of light or power toward the object in question; you can use the wand or athame for this. Alternatively, you can send it into a candle or other article via your hands by cupping the item in your palms and flooding it with energy. This energy can appear as white or golden, or another colour; if you are doing work for healing or growth, you may want to envision it as green.

A group can link hands and begin to draw up energy between them, pushing it mentally from person to person, feeling it begin to spin, visualising it gaining momentum and height. Soon this cone of power will almost become an entity in its own right, picking up speed, growing higher, tapering to a point. The group members should imagine themselves weaving their goals and intentions into this whirling cone of energy so it becomes the vehicle that carries them onto the astral, the plane of being where thoughts take root prior to manifesting on the material level. At some point, one or more of a group will sense that the tension is about to peak and the cone must be released. When this happens, they should signal to let go, at which point people release hands or mentally see the cone of power take off and shoot away, carrying the group magic with it. All this is difficult to describe, but the experience is extremely powerful, leaving the participants with a feeling of exhausted well-being. The optimum time for this type of working is the full moon, when etheric energy is abundant and highly charged. The cone is a potent tool and very likely to bring positive results.

If people want to do any kind of meditation or clairvoyant work, a good time to do this is after sending energy, as everyone will be relaxed and receptive. The cosy womb of the circle is an excellent place for this work, especially for scrying, when a bowl of water, a witch's mirror, or a crystal ball can be passed around.

After this kind of activity, it is time to eat and drink to replenish energy, then end the rite.

Feasting

This is sometimes called cakes and wine, even if no cake or alcohol is consumed. You need some type of drink in the chalice, and bread, cake, biscuits, or something similar to eat.

Hold up the chalice and ask for a blessing on its contents. Say something like:

> **Bless this chalice, Lady, that its contents**
> **may refresh and replenish me.**

You should now drink. Then, if you are in a group, pass the chalice clockwise to the person next to you with the greeting, "Blessed be."

Any food should be placed on the pentacle and held up with a blessing such as:

> **Bless this food, Lord, that it may nourish and**
> **sustain me, grounding me into the world.**

You should now take a portion of food and eat, passing the platter to the next person, saying:

> **Blessed be.**

These are basic blessings, and you will want to use different ones at the festivals, and maybe at the separate moon's phases, described later in the book.

Everybody should take their time to eat and drink and chat before closing the rite.

Ending the Rite

Give thanks to Goddess and God for their presence and bid them farewell.

Go to the eastern quarter and see the yellow light fading, or draw a banishing pentagram, which is the opposite of an invoking pentagram: bottom left to top left, top right to bottom right, diagonally to left side, straight across to right side, diagonally to bottom right, and back up to the top. See the yellow pentagram being taken up until it is gone. Imagine the qualities of air fading back until they return to a normal, everyday state. Say:

> **Powers of the east, powers of air,**
> **thank you for attending.**
> **Hail and farewell.**

Then move clockwise around the circle, doing the same with the other three elements.

It is common at this point for people to say to each other, "Merry meet and merry part, and merry meet again"; and this, along with "Blessed be," has become a much used pagan greeting. On pagan and Wiccan e-mail groups, and in the guest books on pagan websites, people will often begin a message with "Merry meet" (or MM for short) and sign it with "Blessed be" (BB).

It only remains for everyone present to hug each other and then clear up the circle, wash the chalice, bowls, and so on, and put everything away.

Some people like to save a small portion of food and drink to return to the earth as an offering.

This is the framework for all rituals, whether they are lunar or seasonal. It can be adapted and altered, some wording can be changed, some things possibly done in a different order from time to time; for instance, you might sometimes want to invoke Goddess and God before raising energy, or you might do magic in one session but use the next one for meditation or learning a psychic skill such as scrying. But the basic ritual pattern will always be similar. This is the structure that will be fleshed out by developing all the different skills that make up a satisfying and efficient spiritual life.

CHAPTER THREE

The Elements

The elements are the basic building blocks of spiritual and ritual practice, and studying them gives us a better understanding of the world we live in. In the Craft we use them in magic, we use them in circle casting; they are intertwined with the symbolism of the eight seasonal festivals. But just what are the elements, and how do they affect our lives?

The basic elements are *earth, air, fire,* and *water,* but there is a fifth, *ether,* that permeates the others and binds them. They are properties that are present throughout our daily lives, and they are also an important part of astrology and tarot. The astrological signs are divided into: fire, being Aries, Leo, and Sagittarius; earth, which are Taurus, Virgo, and Capricorn; air, which are Gemini, Libra, and Aquarius; and lastly, the water signs of Cancer, Scorpio, and Pisces. The tarot suits are also elemental: wands relate to fire, swords to air, cups to water, and pentacles (or disks or coins) to earth. Fire and air are considered to be masculine, assertive, and outgoing; and water and earth feminine, receptive, and passive, though these "labels" are relative. The elements are also a fundamental part of all religions and spiritual ways. Tibetan Buddhism has the Buddhas of the five directions (including the central direction, which corresponds to ether); the Native American medicine wheel relies on east, west, south, and north, and so on, through all the many spiritual paths. In medieval times the elements were studied seriously as an aid to diagnosing illnesses or mental states, and people were divided into various elemental categories. Within witchcraft we cast the circle, which represents ether or spirit, then we stabilise and centre it by calling in the four quarters, each of which is ruled by a compass direction and an element. The pentagram itself is a symbol for the four basic elements and the binding factor of ether or spirit.

To really get to know the elements, it's a good idea to explore them one at a time in the context within which they naturally occur. This can be done little by little over a period of time, or in a course of deliberate and concentrated study. It's really up to you to decide how you work best. In the following pages I will describe each element in turn and give some suggestions about getting in touch with it. This is something all of us can do; we all have access to the elements, even if we live in a city dwelling with no garden. Do you know anything about your astrological birth chart? This is also a very good way to begin to understand the elements. Using tarot is another.

Earth

I will begin with earth, as witchcraft is an earth religion and therefore this element is extremely important to us. If you live in Europe, then the direction for earth is north, the place of cold, the home of the midnight sun. If you live south of the equator, then earth will relate to south, and fire will be in the north, where the sun is hottest and strongest. The compass directions for the elements are relative and rely on the geographical features where you live. If you have a large land mass to the west of you, then obviously you may not feel comfortable ascribing water to this direction— and may feel it better describes earth instead. For the sake of consistency, though, I will mostly stick to the European correspondences.

Earth is a feminine element; it is stable and sustaining and supportive; it is energy at its most solid; substance; matter; the body of the Great Mother of ancient times. Our bodies are partly made of the earth, belong to the earth, and we return to its embrace when we die, whether whole or as ashes scattered to the four directions. Much of the food we eat comes from the soil, and many things we can touch are made of earth in some way or form. Our physical selves have an intuitive bond with earth, and our ancestors understood this, burying their dead in the womb of the Mother, in caves and burial mounds, with grain and other grave goods beside them. This world of solid matter is the testing ground where we learn and grow and put our discoveries into practice. Money belongs to the earth suit or element, and it is said that money is another form of energy, and that earth is the most spiritual of the elements because it is the one that tests us the most and within which we are able to bring the qualities of the other elements into manifestation. The magical colours for earth are the hues we find in nature: greens, browns, ochre, burnt orange; its season is winter.

Earth qualities are those of dependability, endurance, and stolidness. Think of a mountain, enduring for aeons, only gradually and imperceptibly being worn away. Think of stable, weighty, standing stones, or caverns deep underground, still and quiet. People with a preponderance of earth in their natal horoscopes are usually reliable and practical, the ones to whom we can turn to help us see things through against the odds, because they have inbuilt reserves of staying power. When we want to say that someone is dependable, we often say that they are down to earth or the salt of the earth, though these very qualities of stability and dependability can become stubbornness and inflexibility if carried too far.

Earth is very calm and calming. If we build something lasting, we are drawing on earth. The elemental beings for earth are gnomes (not really little men with green hats— this is a convenient way of symbolising what are really natural forces or energies). The earth element is concerned with all growing things, whether it is the life cycle of a plant or the formation of flesh, teeth, and skeleton in ourselves and other vertebrates. Fire may be life force, air the impulse to thought, and water the emotional response of a sentient being, but earth provides the bricks and mortar.

There are many ways to get in touch with earth, and it's up to you to choose which ones attract you or are the most compatible with the limitations of your individual lifestyle. One very simple way during warm, dry weather is to go into your garden, a field, or your local park, take off your shoes, and walk barefoot on the grass (beware of broken glass). Walk very slowly, feeling the sensation of the ground beneath your feet, the grass, and any small stones or pebbles. After a while you may be able to sense energies coming up out of the ground, maybe making your feet tingle. Take time to experience this. Going barefoot is natural to our species, even if it seems strange at first, and you will find this contact liberating. Remember to attune your senses, to remain open and without expectation. If you are aware of the sensation of earth energies, try drawing them up into your body; you will feel refreshed and replenished. When you are done, ground the excess energy by letting it flow back into the soil; just visualise it flowing out through your feet like trickling water (but don't overdo this or you will drain your own life force— just tell yourself you are dispersing only the excess vital force; trust yourself to know when to stop).

Now go and sit against a tree trunk. Let your attention turn inward and see what thoughts and sensations come to you. This may take a little time so be patient with yourself, and don't worry if nothing seems to happen. Close your eyes if you like; imagine that you are part of the tree and that your feet are really roots that go down into the soil beneath you, drawing up energy, circulating it around your system. See this energy as a moving current of greenish-gold light. After a while, imagine yourself drawing your "roots" back into your feet and disconnecting from the earth and the tree.

Now try lying back on the ground. If you relax you will probably feel the pulse of the earth itself, rather like a heart-beat sounding deep under the soil. Try to imagine the slow growth of plants, the swelling of seeds, and the unfurling of grass and leaves.

If you are lucky enough to have access to one of the ancient sacred sites, go there and see what the experience brings you. Standing stones were placed in such a way that they utilised and intensified the earth currents; and these currents can still be felt very strongly. Touching the stones or even being near them will often allow you to feel quite powerful vibrations. Something similar can be felt at the great ceremonial mounds. At the very least, you will be aware of a special aura or atmosphere at sacred sites.

Bringing flowers into your environment is another way to contact earth. Try to feel their life force even as you enjoy their beauty. Tend plants in your garden or, if you have no green space of your own, on a balcony or in pots around your living space.

Lastly, observe the seasonal changes around you, especially at the times of the eight festivals, when surges of extra earth currents can often be felt. Watch the cycle of growth and decay; see the black branches of trees become tipped with the first thrusting green buds; see the leaves unfurl; follow the cycle through to autumn and the colouring and subsequent falling of leaves; explore the base of tree trunks and see how the foliage is not wasted but rots and mulches down to nourish the growth of future seasons. The earth replenishes and sustains herself and all life that depends upon her.

Here is a beautiful meditation exercise for getting in touch with earth and understanding its powers. Go to a quiet spot, either outside or in an undisturbed part of your home. Place the following on a small table or box or on your shrine (or even on the floor or ground):

- A bunch of flowers
- A bowl of earth
- A similar bowl with salt in
- Green, brown, or deep orange candles, or all three
- Some crystals or stones
- Some bread
- A chalice or cup of red grape juice

Light the candles, then sit comfortably and calmly.

Feel the weight of your own body.

Breathe slowly and deeply, imagining your breath going deeper into your body at each inhalation so you eventually seem to be breathing in and out through your belly. Let your body feel heavier and heavier; just experience the gravity and heaviness of your own flesh and bones.

Look at the candles and "see" the flames weaving a pattern of green or orange or brown (or all of those) so you are surrounded by those earth colours. Try to sense the vital energy of the flowers; touch their petals if you like.

Now pick up the stones or crystals and cup them in your hands, feeling their shape and texture. Hold them to your heart. Do you feel any energy flow? Hold them like that for a while.

Then put them up to your third eye. What images come to you? Don't try to anticipate, but just let impressions come and go as they will.

Put the stones or crystals down and pick up the bowl of soil. Get your hands into the soil, run it through your fingers, rub it over your skin. What does it feel like? Are you aware of its energy? If so, how different is it to the vital force of the stones, crystals, or flowers? Touch some to your third eye. Is this energising or grounding? Do any thoughts, images, or impressions come to you?

Now pick up the bowl of salt. Touch a little of it to your third eye (just above and between your eyebrows), and cup some in the palm of your hand. Does this feel different from the soil? What physical sensations do you feel against your skin? Salt can be very grounding, but in a different way than earth, as it is also used for purification, so you may feel clearer and lighter than you did with the soil. Put a little on the tip of your tongue. I find that doing this instantly grounds me and shuts down my chakras, but you may experience it differently.

Finally, take a piece of the bread, sprinkle it with salt, and eat it, observing how it feels in your mouth, on your tongue. Drink the grape juice.

How do you feel after eating and drinking? Are you more grounded? Did you gain any impressions of the energy that went into growing the wheat and grapes you have just consumed? Think about the soil that grew these crops, the hands that picked them or drove the machinery that harvested them. Feel the food sink into your body, becoming part of you, as you, in turn, are part of the cycle of growth and harvest and decay.

Give thanks to the earth, our Mother, for her gifts.

Put out the candles, bring your attention back to your everyday surroundings, and then write up all you have experienced in your Book of Shadows.

You may do this exercise only once, repeat it as often as you
like, or you can vary it, using it as a basis for your own
exploration.

Water

Except when frozen, water is less solid than earth, though
still denser than fire or air. It is also the most receptive of the
four elements, which is why it has to be cleansed before it
can be used for purification, since it tends to absorb every
nuance of negativity from its surroundings. Water sign people are also receptive, and they have a tendency to take on
the emotional colouring of those around them. Water is very
creative but needs thoughts or inspiration to give it direction, just as it needs to be contained to give it the semblance
of form, or stirred by an outside force to move and change it.
Because of its flowing, seemingly formless nature, water is
often used to symbolise nebulous states such as the psychic
realm or the subconscious.

The direction for water is west, and to the ancient Celtic
peoples this was the direction in which lay the land of the
dead, the Blessed Realm, which was reached over a stretch
of sea. The season ruled by water is autumn, and its time is
twilight or sunset. In Celtic times, water was especially
sacred, and many offerings of swords, chalices, and other
artifacts have been found in lakes and rivers and other bodies of water. Throughout history, water has been seen as a
cleanser; it is used in baptism (to wash away "sin"), in initiation rites, and to purify sacred space, as when cleansing the
perimeter of a Wiccan circle prior to casting. In traditional

coven Wicca, the first initiation is into the feminine ele-33
....
T
H
E

E
L
E
M
E
N
T
Sment of water, which brings us to a symbolic death in the
western quarter and rebirth into the realm of the Goddess,
the Mother, and all things emotional and psychic.

The colours for water are blues, especially violet-blue
and turquoise-blue, and all the bluey-green and greeny-
blue shades. The elemental "beings" for water are undines.
As with the other elements, these are not humanoid creatures, as we sometimes represent them, but forces or energies that we personify in an attempt to better contact or
understand them.

Water is so much a part of our daily lives that we sometimes take it for granted. We have only to turn on a tap to
see it. Next time you fill the kettle or run a bowl of water
for washing, leave the tap running for a while and observe
the way water behaves. As it gushes forth, it displays solid-
seeming, sculptural shapes, taking on the light, and rippling
and spurting according to the pressure and whether or not
you place anything in its flow. Receptive water conforms to
the influences that it encounters.

Although water seems passive, it can be extremely powerful, just as our emotions can overwhelm us uncontrollably at
times. Even on a calm day, the waves pound the seashore with
enormous force, gradually breaking down the coastline and
altering the shape of the land, grinding rocks and pebbles into
sand. If you have ever stood near a waterfall or weir, you will
know how powerful water can be; its sheer volume and pressure could sweep you away, yet it gives you a sense of energy
and exhilaration. Large bodies of fast-flowing water are sometimes used to power electrical generators or drive machinery.
People with a predominance of water in their astrological
makeup can seem passive and yet be extremely tenacious and
persistent—"water wearing away stone." But water is elusive,
too, and just as you can't pin it down to a specific shape,
water-dominated people can appear evasive and indirect.

Yet water is calm and fathomless, like the depths of our unconscious selves. Watching a slow-moving river can calm you, unravelling all tension, bringing a sense of peace and tranquillity, and unlocking psychic receptivity . . . water is an extremely psychic element. One of the most relaxing things we can do is have a bath or go for a swim, because this returns us to the element in which we began our lives in the safety and protection of the womb. Our bodies contain a high proportion of water. All life once came from the sea, and our deep selves remember this and yearn for its comfort. Immersing ourselves in water can put us into an almost trancelike condition, where thought and feeling seem suspended and we enter a state of "just being." Next time you go swimming, let the water carry you, let it support you; experience what it feels like to let go and just float; close your eyes and relax into the embrace of the Mother, she who sustains us all in her womb. When you take a bath or shower, concentrate on the feel of the water moving against your skin, let it caress you and gently wash away the psychic residue of daily life—all the garbage we pick up from other people and our surroundings, the auric pollution that we can't see with everyday vision yet which can drain us and make us feel out of sorts.

We can watch water by observing the weather. Storms drive sheets of rain across the sky; summer rain brings a feeling of release after a hot spell; all nature seems to wake up replenished after rain. Have you ever walked outside during a shower on a warm day? Try it and see how carefree and joyful it can make you feel. Kids understand the pleasure of water play and don't mind getting wet. Tiny babies often love bath time, and older children will play for hours with a bowl of water and a set of containers. Try it yourself, and see how relaxed it makes you feel. One of the summer activities I find most rewarding is skimming fallen leaves and excess pond weed from the surface of our small frog pond; after a while I feel incredibly happy and calm. If you have a pond yourself, or have access to one in a local park, go and sit beside it, gazing into its depths, watching the changing pattern of the sky reflected on its surface or the lazy movements of fish. Feel all tensions quietly leave you. Or sit beside a fast-flowing stream, listen to the water chuckle and gurgle over pebbles and rocks, and see the currents swirl and eddy, streaming the water plants out like hair in a wind.

Try handling pebbles and shells from the seashore. They will retain the energy of the sea and may give you some of their feeling of the ebb and flow of the tides, the constant crash of the waves, and the suck of receding water. Hold them to your third eye and notice the impressions and visions that come to you. Let yourself flow with the experience without expectation. Try wetting the shells or stones and see if that intensifies what you experience . . . it may even revive the odour of the ocean.

To do the following meditation for water, you will need:

- Candles in shades of blue or blue-green
- A bowl of water, preferably spring or mineral water (if you have to use tap water, then cup the bowl in your hands and visualise light streaming from your fingers into the water, cleansing away all negativity and leaving it fresh and clean)
- Some sea salt
- A cup or chalice filled with mineral or spring water, or purified tap water
- A quiet place to sit

Light the candles and let them weave their colours into your consciousness.

Relax and let your perceptions open and your thoughts float gently away.

Breathe easily and slowly, turning your attention inward, away from your surroundings.

When you feel tranquil and calm, take up the bowl of water. Let your hands "feel" the energy of the water within.

Gaze at the surface, possibly seeing the candles or your own face reflected there. Take your time with this and don't try to force any sort of reaction from your senses.

Now dip one finger in the water and dab a little on your third eye, your crown, and your throat. How does this feel?

Carry on holding the bowl, and observe any thoughts, feelings, and visions that come to you, but, again, don't anticipate or force things. Sometimes handling water in this way can release powerful repressed emotions from the subconscious; if this happens to you, allow the process, let it liberate you, then let it all go.

As you relax more and more, gaze deeply into the bowl. You may find you see images, either in the water or in your mind's eye. Or you may simply feel very serene. Whatever happens, view it with acceptance, and don't try to manipulate or push the experience. Water is receptive rather than active—even when it seems to contain force and fury, it is because it is driven by some other factor such as the wind or gravity.

Now take up some of the sea salt and stir it into the water. Do you feel any change in energy? Does this feel more purifying, or more grounding?

Touch your three upper chakras with the salted water and imagine them closing.

Finally, pick up the chalice of water and sip it slowly. Feel the water trickle down your throat, and imagine it eventually flowing through your blood, refreshing your body tissues, cleansing you.

Give thanks to our Mother, in whose womb we all were formed.

Then write up all you felt and experienced.

Remember to dispose of the salted water in a place where it won't damage plants or pollute the soil.

As with earth, you can repeat this exercise if you find it useful to do so, maybe adding to or adapting it to suit your own way of working.

Fire

Finer and quicker than water, yet still denser than air, fire is vital, energetic, and vigorous. Just as fire can leap forth or consume everything in its path, so can fire sign people be passionate, dramatic, and forceful, sweeping everything and everyone before them while their enthusiasm holds sway, only stopping afterward to think of the consequences. Yet fire can be contained and controlled and put to constructive use, both literally and metaphorically. Fire transforms things, making them into something else, whether that means concocting a meal from raw ingredients or effecting a chemical change; when fire is hot enough, even solid rock becomes liquid. Fire was one of the first tools discovered and put to use by our ancestors. It can bring warmth and comfort, but when uncontrolled it wreaks destruction on a massive scale. Fire is also one of the great purifiers, burning away all etheric dross, cleansing sacred space. To many religions, especially the patriarchal Judeo-Christian faiths, it is also a metaphor for spirit. In mythology, smiths are sacred because they shape and transform metal with the aid of fire, symbolising the searing away of our baser selves in the flame of pure spirituality, transforming us into something better.

The direction for fire is south, the place of burning heat, the realm of midsummer and the midday sun. It is a masculine element. Its magical creatures are salamanders, a kind of dragon/lizard creature reminiscent of twisting flames, but, of course, this is personified energy. The magical colours for fire are oranges, golds, reds, fierce yellows. But does fire really display these colours in the natural world? Try watching the flames in a wood or coal fire. Are they really so vibrant and primal, or are they whiter, less saturated? Gas flames are blue, and driftwood also sometimes burns with a blue flame as the salt soaked into it catches alight. Some chemicals burn with a pink or a green flame, and phosphorous is a searing white that will temporarily blind you if you gaze straight at it. The symbolic colours for fire describe its spiritual properties more than its physical ones—they are an exaggeration designed to emphasise the fire qualities of passion, enthusiasm, and ardent creativity.

Fire cannot have existence without fuel to consume, including oxygen. If you want to put fire out, smother it to cut off its supply of air, or douse it with water. In much the same way, people with a lot of fire in their makeup can be suppressed by earthy practicality or watery emotional issues, or starved of incentive if they don't have airy ideas to fuel their driving force. Fire can be emotional, too, of course, but in a very dramatic and passionate manner. Fire people thrive on enthusiasm, and their energy peters out when they run out of fresh issues to become excited about. Yet watching a fire can bring a sense of peace. Have you noticed how lighting candles brings in a sense of the sacred, an inner calm? A lighted hearth brings an atmosphere of comfort, security, and cosiness.

Do you have a fireplace in your home, or a safe place outside where a fire can be kindled? If not, you can light a candle instead. Whatever your source of fire, sit and watch the flames for a while; observe how they shape and change themselves, sometimes flaring up suddenly, sometimes flickering steadily according to whether or not you add fresh fuel, or whether there is a draught, a breeze, or wind. A little wind fans flames to greater activity, but too much can blow them out. If you are burning a fire rather than a candle, see how differently it reacts to coal or wood or paper. But even a candle flame can be fed with a little essential oil or sprinkled with salt (be careful, though—keep the candle in a fireproof container away from loose clothing, draperies, or long, dangling hair). Look at the colours of the flames, and notice how they can be darker at the base, the fuel source, and brighter at the tip. Sometimes it's possible to see pictures in the fire, strange shapes, or images, and this is another form of clairvoyant vision. Be aware of the emotions the fire engenders in you, also. Do you feel revitalised and energetic, passionate or angry, or merely drowsy and snug?

Another way to learn about the qualities of fire is to sit out on a sunny day. The sun is a huge ball of fire and gases, burning with a blue-white radiance rather than the yellow of childrens' drawings (only glance at it, though . . . looking at the sun can be extremely dangerous, possibly leading to blindness). Have you ever noticed how sunshine relaxes us and helps us discard our inhibitions? But too much summer heat can bring tensions and flaring tempers. Sit or lie back with your face raised to the sun and let it play on your closed eyelids, let your skin soak it in. After a while you may feel the fire energy washing over you in slow waves, reaching into your body with each inward breath. It is possible to gain a lot of our energy needs from sunlight alone, and being outside after a long winter can recharge our batteries and bring us a sense of well-being. Let that good energy sink into your skin, your tissues; see the sunlight filtered through the redness of your eyelids. Do you have any thoughts or images as you do this? What does the solar power suggest to you? Do you feel stronger, cheerful, lively, relaxed? Or, conversely, enervated?

How you respond to fire or the sun may depend on where you live and the climate you are used to. If you live somewhere hot and dry, then the sun may be your enemy, bringing drought, discomfort, devastation. To those of us living in moderate to cold climates, both sources of heat are to be welcomed, giving us comfort and warmth on cold days. Western culture draws its idea of hell (in itself a concept alien to witchcraft, I must say) from the desert-dwelling Israelites, on whose religious beliefs Judaism and Christianity are based. To these people, whose lives were lived out in conditions of extreme heat and dryness, the worst environment they could think of was hot and dry, filled with scorching fires. To people who dwell in extremely cold climates, hell may be a place of bitter cold, snow, and ice. Certainly hell as a hot place is a concept that does not match the conditions of northern climates, and I used to draw a great deal of comfort in wintry weather from the thought of the nice warm fires of hell when I was a child!

Preparations for a fire meditation are very simple, and all you need are red, yellow, or orange candles in some kind of holder, and a quiet, undisturbed place to sit, preferably where you will be comfortably warm.

Place the candles in a circle round you, with one in the centre of the circle in front of where you will be sitting, then light them.

Sit calm and relaxed, but alert, and concentrate on the candles, even the ones behind you that you can't see.

Visualise their fiery colours weaving a ring of light and energy around you. Does the space feel different now that the candles are lit, and if so, in what way? Sense the glowing candle flames, feel their quiet power reaching you and enfolding you in their special kind of intensity. Do you feel focused or remote?

Now bring your attention to the central candle. Gaze at its flame for a while, noticing the colours it produces as it burns. You may find that your concentration causes the flame to jump or flicker or spark. Do any images come into your mind, or do you seem to sense any presence behind the candle flame? Do you feel sleepy or alert? Take your time and allow whatever impressions suggest themselves to you. Don't judge.

Reach your hands toward the candle until you can feel its heat on your palms. Visualise yourself drawing the heat and energy in through your fingers, your palms, up your arms, and into your body. What colour is this energy to you? What does it make you feel like?

Continue to draw the energy in on each indrawn breath, feeling it begin to circulate around your system, reaching through your cells and flesh until it irradiates your skin and flows into your outer electromagnetic field, your aura.

Now imagine the energy lighting you up so you seem surrounded by glowing tongues of a fire that soothes and relaxes and revitalises you without searing or burning.

Now see the flames growing smaller, being absorbed through your skin again, their activity becoming quieter and less radiant.

Finally, see any excess energy dying down to a steady glow.

Place your hands on the floor or ground and feel the stability of earth, the solidness of your body.

Thank the God for his gift of fire and for the life force that he gives us.

Then put the candles out and write up your experiences.

Repeat or expand on this exercise if you want to.

Air

Air, which is masculine, is the fastest moving and least dense of the four basic elements, and, accordingly, air-sign people can be restless. It is also the only one of the four worldly elements that is invisible, though we can observe its presence by watching the way it moves the things around us, blowing trees in the wind, fluttering papers on a desk when a door is opened; although, like water, its opposite sign, air can only have power when it is motivated by energy from another source. It is the element most immediately essential to life—as has been said many times before, we can survive for hours without water and days without food, but only a few minutes without air. It is the first element from outside the womb that we take into ourselves at birth, and astrological natal charts should, ideally, be plotted for the time when the first breath is taken (though, in practice, this is seldom done, as it is so difficult to pinpoint that exact time), as this is the time when we let the new life in and accept another term in the world of form. Air is life, and many of us, because of bad experiences or painful challenges, are afraid to take life into ourselves fully, so we breathe from our upper chests only, keeping the breath from penetrating to the depths of our lungs. Magically, air is associated with smoke, especially incense smoke, and it is used as a cleanser via the use of the censer or other incense containers. The lungs are ruled by the air sign of Gemini, and many diseases of the lungs are caused by the air function of smoking.

The direction for air is east and its time is dawn, the time of new awakening and stimulating fresh ideas. Its season is spring. Air colours are pale yellow, pale blue, and clear, light violet. The elemental creatures for air are sylphs, though, as with all the elements, these are not humanoid or animal-like beings, they are energy forms.

In spiritual terms, air is associated with the act of creation, and sound is often believed to be the vehicle through which the manifest world is brought into being. The breath is sacred. The air is not the act of creation itself, but the means via which creation is brought forth. It is the realm of ideas, detached from emotion or action. People who have a lot of air in their makeup appear distant, apart, cerebral, always moving from one idea to another but not necessarily involving themselves with much passion, which can be infuriating to emotional watery types or dramatic fiery folks. Fast-moving modern technologies, such as those used in the communications industry, are related to air, and they can be subject to rapid change and advancement . . . see how quickly the latest computers become outdated (on a monthly basis in many cases) as more and more upgrades and improvements are brought onto the market, yet the technology is seldom completed or perfected because it moves on too fast.

We cannot observe air directly because of its invisibility; we can only see its effects in the world around us. However, we can feel the touch of air in a tactile sense, whether as the gentle caress of a breeze or the power and force of a gale blowing us backward, streaming our hair this way and that, or even the flutter of a breath against our skin. We can watch a field of grass or corn ripple like water as the wind sweeps across it, marvel at the power of wind driven waves, experience fear-tinged exhilaration as clouds are torn and shredded and trees bend over almost double during a storm. Although, when the energy of a fierce wind is spent, everything feels calmer than before, just as expressing our feelings forcefully verbally can bring us a sense of release. If we don't express ourselves, we can often find we have problems with our throats, because the throat is the part of the body through which speech is initiated, and failure to verbalise and communicate can cause a blockage in the throat chakra. Conversely, ideas are best kept unspoken until they have been initiated—vocalising them can dissipate their energy.

An exciting and liberating way to experience the effects of air is to go and stand outside on a windy day. The gusts will cleanse your aura and revitalise you, clearing your thoughts, making you feel fresh and alive and alert. Even if you feel freezing cold, you will still be exhilarated. The east wind can be harsh and sharp, the north wind cold, the south dusty and dry, and the west wind warm and gentle. Of course, these categories are relative to the time of year and weather, but it's surprising how much of the qualities of each element can be carried on each quarter's wind. Thus we can experience the *idea* of each of the elements conveyed through the medium of air.

We can also observe the behaviour of air by watching how it stirs up the other elements in nature. Clouds (which really belong to water) are formed and dispersed by the action of air; water ripples and swirls as the breeze touches its surface; fire bends and flickers or burns steadily according to the air currents; dust or sand is raised by gusts in dry places; birds and other winged creatures move and play as effortlessly in air as do the beasts of its opposite sign of water in their own medium.

Places that are subject to a lot of strong winds have a special energy all of their own, even when the wind is still; and this is especially true of the seashore, hill and clifftop, and open desert or grassland. Here everything feels fresh and alert, vital and clear. Go and stand at the crest of a hill, or on the beach, and feel the clarity of the place; try to observe how that affects you and whether or not you feel more attentive than usual. Pick up any fallen leaves or twigs and see what they have to "say" to you: objects that have been blown by the wind often retain a vigorous, blustery feeling, and wands made from wind felled wood are very powerful tools for raising brisk energy or clearing negative conditions. Being in windy places can give you a sense of cleanliness and lucidity.

To meditate on air you will need:

- A censer or other fireproof container
- A charcoal block (one of the little round self-igniting ones with a depression in the centre)
- Incense, preferably with a light, sharp smell or with lavender as part of the mix (if you don't have the

equipment for burning incense, then a smudge stick or joss sticks will do instead)

- One or more feathers (if you don't have these, then look around outside; they can be found almost anywhere, even in city streets, if you are vigilant)
- Candles in shades of pale yellow, pale blue, pale violet, or all three

Sit somewhere quiet and undisturbed, and light the candles, letting their pale, airy colours penetrate your thoughts.

If it's daytime and you can see the sky from where you are sitting, then this may add to your experience, but it isn't essential.

If you are using incense, then ignite the charcoal; if not, light the joss or smudge stick. When the charcoal is glowing and turning white all the way across (you can accelerate this process by gently blowing across the surface), sprinkle some incense on.

Sit quietly for a while watching the smoke from the incense and breathing in its fragrance. See how the smoke weaves and drifts, making shapes and patterns that may suggest pictures that can be read clairvoyantly. Even in a very still room, smoke will coil and spiral.

Now, lean forward and use one of the feathers to waft the smoke around, seeing how the shapes and patterns change with the increased displacement of air.

Fan the smoke over yourself to clear your aura of any negativity . . . this is an ancient method of cleansing with air and is used during the preparations for casting the circle. Replenish the incense as needed.

Try passing the feather only, without smoke, through the air all round yourself from head to toe, about six inches from your body. How does that feel? Imagine you are sweeping away any psychic debris by stroking the currents of air over your aura. Do you feel cleaner, more alert, or does this action affect you in some other way, and if so, how?

If you have more than one feather, pick the rest up.

Now hold the feather or feathers to your third eye. Do you receive any images, colours, or sensations? Try to sense what it must be like to fly, to be the bird each of your feathers belongs to. Open your mind and let impressions come to you; become a bird yourself for a while; feel the beat of your wings, the pressure of up currents, the whisper of air through your wingtips. Try to imagine what it must be like to spend a large proportion of your life above the surface of the earth, supported only by the air around you.

Finally, bring your awareness back to your earthbound body and the room around you.

Concentrate on your breath, feeling it enter your nostrils and then brush your top lip as you breathe out again. Draw the air deeper and deeper into your body, feeling it expand your lungs. Sit up very straight as you do this so you can give your lungs room to fill properly. Eventually you should be breathing so deeply that your belly expands and then contracts as you breathe.

Visualise the prana (life force) that enters your body with each breath you take. This life force can be seen as bright white light, like sunlight. As you breathe in, concentrate on drawing the prana down into the body, then on each outward breath "see" the pranic energy circulating through your system bit by bit until it reaches the pores of your skin and then your personal force field, until your whole aura is irradiated by light and energy.

Gradually let the light energy fade back, leaving you refreshed but calm.

Put out the candles.

Place the censer, smudge, or joss sticks somewhere safe and let them burn out.

Give thanks to the Sky Father for all you have experienced.

Write up the meditation in your Book of Shadows.

Then go and eat and drink something so you can be certain that you are totally grounded and all your chakras are closed.

As with the other three meditations, you can discard or adapt to suit yourself, and repeat or not as you desire.

Ether

Ether is the fastest moving and least material of all the elements, and it cannot usually be seen at all with normal vision, not even by its effects in the world. It makes up the inner sheath of energy that surrounds us, close to our bodies within our aura, and when we die we experience a later, second death as the etheric or astral form is shed by the outgoing soul.

Ether does not belong to a time or season or compass point, but unites and permeates all of them. It belongs to the centre of the circle, the resting place of being, the apex of the pentagram. It is in the world but hardly of the world, being the energy that surrounds all things in an astral or auric sense. It represents spirit rather than the material world, and yet stands for spirituality in the world of form. Its colour is violet or silvery white.

Ether is the energy that we use to cast a circle, projecting it with our minds out through the point of an athame or wand or finger. We can see it streaming forth from the tip of the athame blade with our psychic or inner vision, though some of us may also *appear* to see the effects with our normal vision as well. This etheric force may be seen as violet or silvery white, or it may be perceived as the colour of the chakra from which we are projecting the energy—very often the yellow of the solar plexus, or a mix of colours if more than one chakra is drawn on.

Etheric energy is also raised involuntarily during large gatherings such as rallies, protest marches, football matches, or rock concerts, where many people share a common emotion; and, of course, it is also intensified by drumming, singing, dancing, or other energy raising methods used in religious gatherings, including Wiccan circles and celebrations. It is also more abundant at some moon phases than others, reaching a peak at full moon—when everybody feels more energetic and "charged"—becoming flatter at the end of the moon's cycle, and peaking again less dramatically at the new moon.

We use ether in magical work, taking steps to increase it within the container made by the sacred circle. It makes up the cone of power that we can build and send to carry our magical intentions, and is the energy source of the charge we project into objects such as candles in order to prime them for spells. It is the most universal of the elements and is everywhere. We use it as a tool to bring change into our lives, whether this is through magical acts or, in a possibly less aware sense, through projecting the force of our emotions into a situation, thus transforming circumstances.

If you want to feel, and possibly "see," the effects of ether, try listening to a piece of music that inspires you or makes you feel charged up. Sometimes, when listening like this, on glancing across the room you may be unable to see clearly because of the increased "texture" of your own aura swirling in front of your vision. Try glancing with half-closed eyes to increase the possibility of seeing this phenomenon.

People can become overexcited when they experience increased amounts of etheric energy through music or dance,

and this can leave them feeling irritable until the excess
drains away. Etheric charge also opens the chakras, so a
group of people undergoing the same emotional event will
experience a mingling of auric force and, consequently, very

similar if not identical responses and understanding. This
happens very often in the witches' circle when everyone
present will have extremely similar perceptions and emotions and will feel especially attuned to each other, and this
is one reason that practicing ritual together bonds the participants over a period of time.

A deficit of etheric energy will make us feel drained and
out of sorts, emotionally and physically low; this is one reason why it's important, during magical work, to draw in
etheric energy from outside ourselves, rather than using up
our own supply.

To experience ether, sit somewhere quiet and dimly lit and
have incense and violet or silver-coloured candles burning.

Gradually relax and deepen your breathing until everyday
thoughts start to fade away and you feel calm.

Now begin to sense the connection between your body and
the ground; feel the contact points between them; imagine
yourself "rooted" to the spot, but not immovably so; you
can get up and move around at any time you wish to.

As you breathe in, feel yourself drawing up energy from the
earth beneath you (even if this earth is deep under concrete or several stories below you in the building where
you sit).

Visualise more energy flowing into you from the air around
you; see it being drawn in through your nostrils, your skin,
your fingertips. You may feel this indrawn energy as a tingling that starts in your fingers and gradually travels up
your arms and into your body, or floods through your air-
ways and makes your head centres feel refreshed and vital.

Now briskly rub your hands together, then bring them gradually toward each other. You should find there is a point at which you experience a bouncy, rubbery type of resistance because your etheric sheath has been charged and is acting rather like a force field that prevents your hands from coming together.

Hold your hands up in front of your face and look at them away from a light source, with half-closed eyes. Can you see anything? (If you can, you may perceive this in your mind's eye.) Don't try to anticipate what you think you should be seeing, but remain open-minded.

Imagine that you are gathering the force from around your hands, focusing it into a ball of energy, gradually transferring this energy to your dominant hand (usually the one you write with).

Point your index finger and push the energy with your mind, seeing it begin to flow out through your finger in a steady stream of light. What does this feel and look like? What colour do you perceive the light to be? Don't worry if you don't seem to be able to visualise this properly. What do your other senses tell you? Do you feel any tingling or change in temperature around your hands? Take your time, projecting the stream of light into the room.

As you do this, gather more energy from around you, channeling it through your body and out through your finger, and as you do so, begin to move your hand so that you are drawing a line of "light," rather like somebody drawing with a sparkler or pen torch. Visualise strongly how this line of light appears. Is it thick or thin, bright or dull, and what colours does it have?

Finally, pull the energy back toward you and reabsorb it into your finger, drawing it up into your body. See any excess energy trickling away through your body-to-floor contact points.

When you feel stable and centred, write up your experiences.

Now that you have experienced the elements individually, it's time to increase your understanding of them through a simple exercise that puts them together. The first thing you need to do, if you don't already know, is to work out the orientation of the four directions in the space you are using. The simplest way to do this is with a compass. If you don't have a compass and don't want to buy one, you will have to consult a map of the area or ask other people.

For the exercise you will need the following supplies:

- A bowl, cup, or chalice of water
- A bowl of earth or compost
- Incense, either in stick form or to be used on a charcoal block in a censer
- Five candles: one green, one blue, one red, one yellow, and one violet or silver

Light the green candle and place it in the northern quarter of the room, out at the edge of the useable space, with the bowl of earth in front of it.

Light the yellow candle and place it in the eastern quarter.

Then get the charcoal going and put plenty of incense on it, placing the censer by the yellow candle.

Place the lighted red candle in the south, then the blue candle and the bowl of water in the west.

Lastly, light the violet or silver candle and put that in the centre of the circle, in front of your sitting space.

Sit comfortably in the circle's centre, breathe steadily and deeply, but without straining, then feel yourself rooted where you are, with energy entering your body from the earth and the air around you at every indrawn breath.

When you feel relaxed but alert, turn your attention to where you are . . . exactly where you are . . . in relationship to the four elements and candles you have placed at the perimeter of your space. You are at the centre. Feel that fact; imagine that you are at the hub of a wheel that is slowly turning around you in time and space, so that earth, air, fire, and water, north, east, south, and west spin on the world axis, each presenting itself to you in turn. Feel the lines of force that connect you to the four basic elements. In your mind, as each element comes round, concentrate on it, visualising all the qualities you have learned to associate with it. See the colours each element has, and let those colours fashion themselves into a spiral that weaves itself around you, twirling higher and higher as the wheel turns.

After a while, let the wheel become stationary. Send your consciousness out, one at a time, to each of the quarters, and imagine that there is a channel of energy connecting you at your central point to each element: green for earth, yellow for air, red for fire, and blue for water. See these channels of energy as glowing and alive. Visualise the qualities of each element flowing toward you along these lines of energy, into you at the centre, the place of ether, of spirit.

Then let the fifth element, ether, flow out to each of the other four. Ether is the centre, but it is the circumference also, and it is everywhere. See the ether as silvery or violet light, which does not dilute the hue and saturation of the other elemental colours.

Think about what it could mean for something to be the centre of everything and yet be everywhere else as well: this is a metaphor for our own spirituality and symbolises the fact that we are always at the centre of everything; we are home at all times, wherever our physical location might be . . . the centre of the universe is within our own being. This is a fact that cannot be reasoned but only understood intuitively.

As you sit there, try to look inside yourself, into your own centre. Try to imagine that everything that ever was or is or will be is contained inside you: all those you love, or don't love; every tree and animal, bird and rock and flower; slugs, snails, butterflies; sun, rain, snow, and the turning seasons; every good act and bad that anyone has ever committed; all moments of peace or conflict . . . everything that makes up the totality of experience as we know it. Embrace these things, for they are part of you. This is the centre of the circle, the heart of the mandala, the apex of the pentagram, all of which are represented by ether.

At last, turn your attention outward again, into the outer world, in which we live our everyday lives.

Visualise yourself drawing the energies of the five elements into yourself, balancing your way of being.

Touch the floor, pat your legs, then write up your experiences before eating or drinking to make sure you are properly grounded.

Hopefully, exploring the elements, or even reading about them, will give you a better understanding of the way they contribute to our lives and can be incorporated into ritual practice. It's important to realise that the way each of us perceives or understands any aspect of spirituality is very personal. I have described the colours and qualities of the elements as I have learned them or interpreted them over the years. You may have a different way of seeing. There are many occult systems, each with its own set of correspondences. There are many individual ways of seeing, too, so while one person may instinctively think of water as blue, another may see it as green or silver or brown, and so on with the other elemental colours and qualities. You must use what works best for you—though bear in mind that correspondences in frequent use will have built up a lot of power on the astral level over many centuries and will therefore be easier to work with; and sometimes, especially if you are going to do a lot of ritual with others, it's easier to use the associations that most people are familiar with.

One last suggestion regarding integrating an understanding of the elements is to set up a special altar to them, or bring objects related to them onto your personal shrine. It is quite common for people to have examples of the elements on their shrines and altars in the form of a bowl of water or shells for water, salt or soil or plants for earth, candles for fire, and incense or feathers for air. You can also set up individual displays for each element, using only associated objects and colours for each one, placing these specialised shrines in the corresponding quarters.

Having a special place for a particular element can also be helpful if you want to develop its qualities within yourself or come to understand it better, and an extension of this would be to make use of its particular colours, too, perhaps in clothes or furnishings. For example, an anecdote for sluggishness and lack of energy could be to concentrate on fiery colours for a while, using red and orange on your shrine and burning fiery-coloured candles, and this could be extended to wearing at least one article of warm-coloured clothing, and perhaps eating orange and red foods, such as peppers.

There are many, many ways to explore the elements. The important thing is to understand that they are a fundamental part of life in the world, but are also our interface with the sacred.

CHAPTER FOUR

Chakra Work

When we are pursuing psychic work such as clairvoyance, healing, magic, and the performance of ritual, including casting the circle, we use our chakras. Within our bodies, there is a constant drawing in and giving out of energy, either through all chakras simultaneously or through one or two that are particularly involved with our current activity.

Each of us is surrounded by an energy field, the aura, which stands out several inches from our physical body. People who are gifted in reading the aura can tell our current state of mind, whether we are well or not, how tired we are feeling, and whether we are calm or angry, sad or elated. Not all of us possess the gift necessary to read the aura this well; however, all of us can learn to see its energies, which can be perceived as swirling, coloured light.

The chakras are points on the aura, connected to our physical bodies, where the light grows brighter, more intense. Each chakra is concerned with a different function of life. Chakra is a Sanskrit word meaning "wheel"—so named because these centres are often seen as spinning disks of energy. They are sometimes called lotuses instead. There are seven major chakras and many minor ones—including those found on the palms of the hands, the soles of the feet, and behind the nipples. However, most spiritual systems concentrate on the major seven.

Each chakra has its own colour and function, though the correct colours can become dull or muddy or pale if we are undergoing any sort of mental, emotional, physical, or psychic stress. Conversely, happy states, or creative work, sex, and ritual will intensify the brightness of the aura and the chakras and deepen their colours.

Furthermore, blocks or imbalances in a particular chakra can lead to illness in the parts of the body associated with that centre.

The chakra colour system we have learned in the West is red for the base or root chakra, orange for the sacral or navel chakra, yellow for the solar plexus chakra, green for the heart chakra, blue for the throat chakra, violet for the third eye or brow chakra, and white for the crown chakra. However, the Hindu system is different, and the following is a brief description of the names and colours it assigns these centres, working upward from the base or root chakra. Note that each chakra is assigned a number of petals (because the chakras are seen as lotuses) and a mantra or sacred sound (also a set of deities, not mentioned here). The whole system is extensive and complex, but well worth further study, not least because it was the original basis for the chakra work we do in the West.

Muladhara Chakra

Colour: yellow

Element: earth

Number of petals: four

Sound: Lam

Svadhishthana Chakra

Colour: white

Element: water

Number of petals: six

Sound: Vam

Manipura Chakra

Colour: red

Element: fire

Number of petals: ten

Sound: Ram

Anahata Chakra

Colour: grayish-blue

Element: air

Number of petals: twelve

Sound: Yam

Vishuddha Chakra

Colour: greenish-blue

Element: ether

Number of petals: sixteen

Sound: Ham

Ajna Chakra

Colour: white

Element: mind

Number of petals: two

Sound: Ohm

Sahasrara Chakra

Colour: all colours and no colour

Number of petals: a thousand (but meaning infinite)

Element: cosmic consciousness, experience of being one with all creation

Sound: all sounds and no sound

The Tibetan system is slightly different again, and they double up the third eye and crown chakras and see them as one.

Working with the chakras is an essential part of witchcraft, though many people use them without being aware of the fact, or may know chakra activity is taking place but may ignore it or take it for granted. To be efficient, it isn't necessary to work consciously with the chakras, but it can help to balance our energy flow and strengthen our aura, which in turn keeps us better protected from outside interference as well as other people's negative thoughts and emotions. Know that if you are meditating, doing ritual work, listening to music, and so on, your chakras will be open (though you may be unaware of the fact), and *you* will be open . . . to others' energies, to the full impact of whatever activity you are involved in. This is why it is so important to close the chakras after psychic activity. Eating is the quickest and simplest method of closing down, and the feast at the end of a rite has the dual purpose of celebration and shared communion, and grounding one and closing one's auric centres. If you don't do this, you are leaving yourself vulnerable to whatever is around you, and you will eventually feel very lightheaded and drained. If you are continually wide open to the thoughts and feelings of others, you may become confused about who you are as well as your own motivations.

The following is a brief description of the chakras, their locations and functions, as commonly understood in Western magical and spiritual systems. They can be located from either the front or the back of the body, being seen as sited along the spinal column if the latter (with the exception of the crown chakra), though their energies overlap into broader areas of the body. I will describe them as though looking at the spine, but will give the front of the body placements as well.

The Base or Root Chakra

Seen from the back of the body, this chakra corresponds with the coccyx, which is the little nub of bone, the residual tail, in which the spine culminates, though its specific site is the perineum, radiating out to the external sex organs. It should be deep, rich, fiery crimson-red in colour, but depletion will drain it to a paler shade, and anger or ill health may deepen it to maroon, or tinge it with brown.

This chakra is concerned with our connection to the physical world, and is ruled by earth. It governs the outer organs of reproduction, the feet, the spine, the kidneys, and the anus. It has an influence on our ability to survive, to stay healthy, and to connect to our basic drives. Working with it will increase vigour, vitality, and the sense of belonging in the world of form.

The Sacral or Navel Chakra

Located a little way below the waist, encompassing the small of the back and the area just below the navel, this is the centre that connects us to our emotions and our sexuality. It is ruled by water. It should be bright, vibrant orange in colour, but ill health or negativity will turn it a sludgy hue, and tiredness will bleach it paler orange or tinge it with gray. It is associated with the inner reproductive organs and the urinary system.

This centre helps us to channel our material needs and wants; if we block ourselves here, then we live in straightened circumstances; if we work on this chakra or allow it to flow, we can bring abundance into our lives . . . one reason why vibrant orange is a good colour choice for magic involving money or prosperity. If we centre ourselves here, rather than the upper chakras, then we will feel much more balanced and serene.

The Solar Plexus Chakra

A radiant, sunny yellow, this chakra is located between the waist and the bottom of the shoulder blades, and the midriff section below the breast bone. It is ruled by fire, and its health and state affect our self-determination and will power. Tension or nervousness will tighten it and make us feel churned up and jittery, maybe even sick. Illness can taint its colour to murky olive, while depletion drains it to pale yellow. If we refuse to express anger, then we may hold it in here, eventually leading to depression and edginess.

Working on this chakra can help us to release anger and tension as well as to feel more in control of our lives. In general, it governs the gallbladder, liver, and digestive system.

The Heart Chakra

Located between the shoulder blades at the back of the body and the breasts at the front, this chakra should be a deep, clear emerald or grass-green color, though sadness will turn it grayer, tiredness will pale it, and negative emotion and grief will turn it dark and muddy. It governs the heart, blood, and circulatory system.

Ruled by air, this is the chakra most concerned with love and compassion. When we act from this chakra, we act from the heart and put others before ourselves. It is also the middle chakra, and so unites the upper and lower centres. When we are in tune with the heart, we don't live only by our baser instincts and for self-gratification, neither do we live in a lofty spiritual world out of touch with reality; instead, we experience our spirituality and creativity through the body and the world we live in, and through other people. Working with this chakra teaches us to love fully and deeply; and this includes loving ourselves.

The Throat Chakra

This chakra is located at the base of the neck and in the hollow above the collar bones, and is a glowing sky-blue. It is concerned with vibration and sound, creativity and the ability to express oneself, especially verbally. It rules the lungs, respiratory system and throat, vocal chords, jaw, and mouth. If it is blocked, we may have trouble with the throat, or may be unable to speak up for ourselves or express our feelings freely. If we are explaining heartfelt emotions, then its colour may deepen to peacock blue as the green of the heart chakra is brought up and released as speech.

Working with this chakra can help to release deep-seated shyness and inarticulateness. Our voices can gain in power and become very compelling and moving. We will also gain confidence in situations in which we have to speak in public or we need to justify ourselves verbally. Ritual invocation will also help this chakra to develop and to stay clear.

The Brow Chakra or Third Eye

This violet-coloured chakra can be found just above the hollow at the base of the skull and the space between the eyebrows. It is concerned with sight, both physical and psychic, and with the ability to visualise . . . clairvoyance is a function of the third eye, as is clairaudience. It also governs the ears, nose, and nervous system. Through the third eye, we see beyond our limiting material circumstances; we can look both backward and forward, peruse the whole cloth, so to speak, rather than our small piece of the pattern, attaining a cosmic overview.

Working too much with this chakra, without the balance of the others, can make us feel dizzy and disoriented or lead to headaches and migraines. Absorbing negative thoughts and feelings from others will tinge it with gray or a redder purple, while exhaustion will turn it a dull, light lavender.

Using this centre positively will increase our visual creativity and psychic abilities in general. It may also sharpen our physical vision and hearing.

The Crown Chakra

This centre is brilliant white and is situated above the crown of the head. It governs the brain and connects us to the universal whole (just as the base chakra roots us into the worldly plane of being). Through the crown chakra we can experience *samadhi* or cosmic consciousness, where we move beyond individuality to our interconnectedness with all of life and the meaning of existence. We no longer feel the need to attain, but are content just to be. It is an experience beyond concepts of time and space, and yet it encompasses all we have ever been and known.

When this chakra is blocked, we cannot "spread our wings"; we remain locked into our own problems and misery with no understanding of why. But working with the crown chakra brings understanding and liberation, a sense of belonging, the knowledge that we are not alone, and all is well.

Please note that some systems use indigo as the colour for the third eye, and violet for the crown. The best way to work with chakra colours is to try out different systems and see what feels most comfortable for you; though be careful that you don't assign a colour to a chakra and then find you had perceived it that way because an imbalance in that specific chakra in your own auric field had clouded your perception.

Chakra Exercises

There are many different ways to work with the chakras, and each proponent has his or her own ideas. Eventually, people find a way that suits them. I have found the following exercises helpful over the years when doing healing or balancing work with people, or when teaching them to open and close the chakras during ritual and meditation. Remember, if you are happy with the way you work and don't feel you need to explore the chakras further, then that's okay. For those who want to go deeper, try these exercises and then use the ones with which you are most comfortable, or use them as a starting point for your own work.

Some people will find that the chakras open quickly and easily, so that the next colour starts to impinge on consciousness almost before the last chakra is fully opened; others will have to work harder, and may need several attempts at an exercise before they feel they are getting somewhere; these variations in experience happen because of differing levels of familiarity with ritual or psychic work and meditation, states of tiredness or health at a given time, and many other factors. Some chakras may respond more quickly than others, possibly indicating places where we are blocked or have a weakness. None of these variations are ultimately important since regular chakra work will get the energies flowing freely and balance the whole aura.

Rainbow Chakra Exercise

Go at your own pace with this exercise (as with all of them), moving on to each chakra when you sense the last is fully open and active.

Sit somewhere comfortable, where you will be undisturbed. In front of your altar or shrine might be an ideal place. Draw the curtains if it's still daylight outside, and light candles and incense. Some authorities advocate playing music; personally, I find it a distraction, but if you find it helps you to concentrate then put on something soothing.

Breathe calmly and deeply until you feel centred, then close your eyes.

Visualise your feet being rooted to the ground. Imagine the earth energies beneath you and begin to draw them up into your body. "See" these energies as a stream of brilliant white or silvery light, which begins to travel up your legs to your spine.

At the base of the spine is a small, glowing red disk, and as the light reaches it, the disk grows larger and glows a deep, fiery red (it may help to see this disk or wheel of red whirling faster as it takes up the light). Try to make a mental note of how the energy of the root chakra makes you feel.

When the red wheel is glowing and spinning satisfactorily, carry on drawing up white light until you reach a point around the small of the back where the sacral chakra is situated. See the orange disk of the sacral chakra expand until it is a whirling ball or wheel of bright orange light, and note what this feels like.

Carry on drawing up the white earth energy until you reach the solar plexus chakra, between waist and shoulder blades, and let that centre expand also, until it is a glowing disk of radiant yellow.

Continue in the same manner to the heart chakra, and let the small green disk open out into a whirling circle of intense emerald green; note how this makes you feel.

Carry on to the throat chakra, letting the white light flood it and energise it until it is a vital centre of luminous sky blue.

Carry the same energy up to the brow chakra and let it expand and increase until it, too, is a pulsing circle of light, filling the space between the eyes and at the back of the head with radiant violet-purple.

Let the white energy flow up through the crown of the head to irradiate the crown chakra itself, flooding it with intense white light.

When the crown chakra is thoroughly activated, let the light fountain out and around, forming a circle of light round the body until you are surrounded. Visualise this circle of light forming a rainbow around you, containing all the colours of the chakras. Let this energy play around you for a little while, revitalising you, cleansing your aura.

Imagine the rainbow of energy gradually withdrawing, being absorbed back through the crown of the head, flowing downward again.

As the stream of light leaves the crown chakra, see the chakra becoming less active until it is a smaller, white, glowing ball above the head, but leave it a little open so that you are still connected to the cosmos. The crown and base chakras are always left slightly open in this way to maintain our connection to earth and sky.

Let the stream of white light sink down from the crown chakra to the level of the third eye, and see the violet wheel of energy gently closing down until it is a small, glowing disk of violet again.

Continue like this down through the chakras, closing each one as you go.

When you get to the base chakra, let the wheel of red become smaller but not completely closed, leaving a connection with the worldly plane.

Let the earth energy sink down, right back down to the feet, then mentally disconnect from the earth, open your eyes, and become aware of your everyday surroundings.

When you are ready, write about your experiences.

Chakra Balancing

This is a very useful exercise if you are feeling drained, tense, or off balance in some way.

Sit somewhere peaceful and calm, draw the curtains, and light candles and incense if you wish.

Breathe slowly and regularly until you feel calm and tranquil, then close your eyes.

Concentrate on the area where the sex organs meet the top of the thighs, encompassing the area up to the pubic line, visualising glowing red light. You don't have to see this as a sphere or disk. If this red area looks muddy or pale, concentrate on making it a true, rich red; don't move on until it is the correct colour and is glowing with light and energy.

Move up toward the navel and see an area of bright orange encompassing the whole region of the lower abdomen. Examine the colour and brightness of this area, and don't move on until it is a pure, radiant orange.

Move up into the glowing yellow light around the solar plexus, below the breast bone, and work on visualising the correct sunny yellow if this area seems pale or murky in colour.

Move up to reach the point between the breasts, where the light is a true emerald green; if the colour is too dark or pale, or is mixed with other hues, then work on it until it is the right shade and tint.

Come up to the blue at the base of the throat, noting any grayness, dullness, or other unwelcome variations, visual-ising the clearest rich sky blue before moving on.

Move to the violet purple of the third eye. Note any discrep-ancies in hue and shade, and work on seeing the area between the brows and onto the forehead as a rich, deep violet.

Come to the crown of the head and see brilliant white light reaching up above the crown. There must not be any other colours mixed in, only bright, flawless white, so work on eliminating any colour casts.

Now let the white light reduce to a smaller, glowing area above the head, but don't close it down completely.

Return to the third eye and let the violet light fade to a small area.

Go on down the body, closing the chakras by letting them become very small again, except for the base, which needs to be left slightly open for connection to the physical world, just as the crown stays slightly open to keep us con-nected to the cosmos.

Finally, open your eyes and come back to your normal surroundings.

You may need to do this exercise several times to thoroughly cleanse and balance the chakras, returning them to
their correct colours; so be prepared to repeat the exercise
on two or three or more consecutive days.

Cleansing and Grounding Exercise

This exercise can be done anywhere, and need only take a
little while. It is especially useful when you have been doing
activities such as dashing around, studying, or pursuing some
matter on the phone (all of which concentrate energy in the
head at the expense of general equilibrium). It will help you
to feel more grounded and less tense or spaced out. It can
also help if you are feeling strung out after psychic activity.

Sit or stand as relaxed as you can.

Imagine that your feet are rooted to the ground; really visualise the earth, even if you are high up in a building or
standing on concrete.

Visualise a gentle rain trickling down on your head, washing
your crown clean, soothing you, closing your crown
chakra down to its everyday state.

Feel the rainwater trickling down from your head, down your
forehead, over your closed eyes, over your third eye,
cleansing and soothing it, closing it if it is open, giving
you a rest from psychic receptivity.

Down your nose, over your lips, your chin, your throat, and
across the throat chakra, washing it clean, calming it,
soothing it, closing it, letting your voice be stilled for a
little while.

Down over your collarbones and upper chest until it is gently soothing and cleaning your heart centre, healing any hurts, letting pain and constriction loosen and seep away, closing your heart centre gently to its everyday state.

Down to the solar plexus, loosening tension, gently and quietly flushing out anger or distress, fear or apprehension, washing it all away, closing the centre.

Down to the navel, cleansing away feelings of self-doubt, balancing you, grounding you, closing activity down for a while.

Down to the base chakra, washing away tiredness, exhaustion, ill health, leaving you vitalised but serene.

Trickling over your thighs, your knees, your calves, your ankles, down to your feet to flow away into the good earth, taking all that tension and negativity with it, giving it all to the Mother to cleanse.

Draw your awareness back into your feet, then have a warm drink or something energising, like fruit, to eat.

Crystal Chakra Cleansing

For this you will need a single clear quartz crystal. It needs to be very clean, so soak it for at least three hours, but preferably overnight, in a container of water and sea salt (dissolve about a tablespoon of salt in a pint of water). When you retrieve the crystal, pour the water away down the sink and ask that any negativity be transmuted into clean, positive energy. Then rinse the crystal under the tap, visualising it being washed by a mountain stream or a waterfall as you do so.

You need to be a little wary when working with crystals, unless you have a lot of experience with using them. Crystals, and especially clear quartz, amplify energies, so it's not a good idea to project white light or strong emotions through them, as is suggested in some books, unless you are sure of what you are doing, not least because working in such a way can cause quite a traumatic release of emotion and bottled-up feelings, which, though ultimately cathartic, may be overwhelming and hard to cope with. For this exercise, you need to use the crystal to suck up negativity rather than to direct a cleansing ray into the chakras. Careless misuse of a crystal could possibly damage your subtle bodies and leave a small breach in your auric shield . . . not probable but possible, and, therefore, worth being cautious about.

Sit somewhere comfortable, relaxing, and quiet, where you won't be disturbed.

Hold the crystal point down a few inches above the crown of your head. Keep it there until you sense you should move on. You don't need to imagine it drawing any negativity into itself, as it will do this of its own accord. You may feel a tugging, as though something is pulling at your scalp. You may feel a tension followed by a sense of release or relief; you may want to cry, or you may feel elated. All these things are symptoms of psychic residue leaving the chakra. This is the general gunk that we pick up from our surroundings and the people we interact with on a daily basis. Regular chakra work will build up a lot of protection against absorbing this kind of stuff.

Gently bring the crystal down until it is pointing at your third eye, two or three inches away from the point between your eyebrows, and follow the same pattern, moving on when you feel you should. You may again feel tension followed by release.

Point the crystal at the base of your throat, holding it a couple of inches away. You might find that you want to cough or clear your throat, and this, again, shows that the chakra is becoming freed of unwanted residues.

Go down to the point between the breasts and cleanse the heart chakra. Releasing blockages here will result in a feeling of deep love and compassion welling up.

Now work in the same way on the other chakras, holding the crystal a little closer for the solar plexus, sacral, and root chakras.

Your chakras will now be cleansed but open. A quick and effective way of closing them after this type of work is to visualise yourself being surrounded by a cloak of green or deep-blue energy.

Lastly, go and eat something to make sure the chakras are totally closed and you are properly grounded. It's a good idea to cleanse the crystal in salt water again to remove any residue of negativity left over after the cleansing exercise.

When cleansing the chakras, you may sometimes find that a blockage in one is caused by taking in negativity through another centre. You may find that a chakra stubbornly refuses to release its block until you move on to the others, when you will suddenly feel a release occur in the earlier chakra as well. The solar plexus and third eye can sometimes be paired in this way, or the throat and third eye.

I have described just a few methods of cleansing and balancing the chakras. The important thing to realise is that we should work with all the chakras in harmony. If you single out only one, you will cause an imbalance in your energies, unless, of course, you are clearing a block or building up a centre that is weaker than the others. Beginners to occult work often want to concentrate solely on opening the third eye or working with the crown, but this leads to giddiness, faintness, disorientation, tension, or lethargy. If you are doing a lot of clairvoyant work, balance it by eating sensibly and exercising, reading, and talking. Don't concentrate on one or two centres and ignore the rest. The upper two or three chakras are not more spiritual than the others, and we need to use them all in harmony to be properly realised individuals.

Working with Crystals and Stones

Each of the chakras has crystals, semiprecious stones, and gemstones associated with it. If you want to clear stubborn blocks in a specific chakra, or strengthen a chakra, you can carry minerals of the appropriate colour, or lay them on the associated area of the body. The following is a fairly comprehensive list of suitable minerals to use:

Base Chakra

Smoky quartz; jet; obsidian; black tourmaline; red jasper; ruby; garnet.

Navel Chakra

Deep orange citrine; orange topaz; deep-shaded amber; carnelian.

Solar Plexus Chakra

Yellow citrine; light-shaded amber; yellow topaz; yellow diamond.

Heart Chakra

Emerald; dioptase; green, pink, or watermelon tourmaline; peridot; kunzite; rose quartz; green jade; rhodochrosite (some of these stones are pink, which is another heart chakra colour).

Throat Chakra

Lapis lazuli; turquoise; aquamarine; blue sapphire; blue topaz.

Brow Chakra

Lapis lazuli (note that the mixture of colours in this stone makes it appropriate for both throat and brow); indigo sapphire; amethyst; sodalite; luvulite.

Crown Chakra

Clear quartz; diamond; white topaz; white sapphire; white jade.

As I have mentioned before, if you are doing psychic, creative, or spiritual work, including magic and ritual, then you will be using and developing the chakras. However, choosing to work on them in a more informed way may be useful as an aid to righting blocks and imbalances, and in strengthening certain centres that need to be brought into line with the rest; all this will happen eventually, gradually, and naturally, generally just by doing ritual work, but it may be useful to take more control of the process. It will certainly be interesting.

CHAPTER FIVE

Meditation and Visualisation

Meditation is an important part of spiritual practice to many witches, an activity that can be an aid to harmony and balance, to spiritual development, or to enhancing visualisation and receptivity, which in turn develop the efficiency of ritual and magic. But it is an activity that is subject to many different interpretations, and some people like to incorporate a meditation session into ritual, while others keep it separate.

Meditation is not, as many people mistakenly believe, a matter of making your mind blank, then using willpower to keep out any thoughts, something that is almost impossible to achieve and that would destroy any hope of attaining tranquillity or spiritual insight. In fact, meditation is far more effortless and natural than that, and develops willpower and discipline as a welcome side effect rather than as a technique (though you have to have enough self-discipline and incentive in the first place to set aside time and space to do it).

There are three main branches of meditation in general use: the first, which is Buddhist in origin, is mindfulness/insight meditation, and the other two, which stem from the Western mystery tradition, are visualisation and guided meditation/pathworking. I use these definitions rather loosely; the categories cross over, and all share or utilise techniques common to the others. The best way to explain them is to describe them in action. I have used all of them over the years, though I don't often use guided meditation because I don't find it as effective as the other methods—some other people, however, do find it helpful, so try it out and see if it works for you.

Whichever methods of meditation you try, you need to practice in a place where there are few distractions. You also need to be comfortably seated, but with your back straight and relaxed. Sit in one of the cross-legged postures, if possible. The lotus or half-lotus would be ideal, but not all Westerners can manage it. An ordinary cross-legged pose is okay, though you may find you get pins and needles after a while. An alternative is to straddle a special meditation stool or cushion, or a thick pillow, knees taking your weight. Or sit in a chair with your feet flat on the ground.

Buddhist Meditation

There are several branches of Buddhism, among them Theravada Buddhism and Zen, and they each approach meditation in a slightly different manner, though the aim is the same in each case: to attain tranquillity, insight into the meaning of life, and/or eventual liberation from the world of form. Although witches honour the earth and our time in the world, considering the gift of worldly existence precious and sacred, and, therefore, aren't particularly looking for release from it, nonetheless, learning Buddhist meditation can be very useful to us: it helps us to become calmer, more centred, and more able to cope with what life throws at us, and it gives us profound insights into how we interact with the rest of life, and how our energies and minds function. The way this type of meditation works is to gradually still the chattering, everyday mind so that it no longer holds centre stage, thus allowing deeper insights and realisations to come into consciousness. This process is sometimes likened to the way the clouds clear to leave the purity of the sky and allow the power of the sun to beam forth.

Mindfulness of Breathing

Find a quiet spot, light candles and incense, and have flowers or a plant in the meditation space.

Sit as described earlier.

Close your eyes and begin to breathe calmly and deeply.

Concentrate on your breath, observing the inward and outward flow of air.

If you start to think about something else, bring your attention gently but firmly back to your breathing. Don't judge yourself or feel you have failed if your mind strays; simply note what it was that distracted you and then come back to observing your breath.

If you hear distracting sounds, like activity outside, or your tummy gurgling, make a brief mental note and then come back to the breath. Similarly, if you are uncomfortable, pay brief attention to the itch or ache, and then come back to your breathing. Many aches and pains will disappear once you acknowledge them, but if they don't, then deal with them (scratch the itch, move the cramped limb) quietly and calmly, and return your attention to your breathing. The idea is to observe without judgment.

You aren't in competition with yourself, or trying to prove anything, you are just allowing things to be as they are without engaging your rational mind.

Now bring your attention to your nose and top lip. Feel the breath as it flows into your nostrils, and then the sensation as it flows out again, brushing your lip as it does so. Sometimes concentrating on the breath here may cause your breathing to slow right down or appear to cease altogether, and this is a sign that you are deeply concentrating and rising above distractions. Don't panic, you aren't going to suffocate; in fact, the experience can be very calm and detached.

After a while, follow the breath deep into your body, feeling the rise and fall of your stomach, following your breath right down into your body and out again several times.

All the time, keep bringing your attention back to your breath if it strays.

Finally, detach your attention from the breath, open your eyes, and reconnect with your surroundings.

Practiced over a period of time, this type of meditation will bring a sense of being very calm and poised, very clear-headed. Eventually, deeper insights will start to arise during meditation sessions, and when they do they should be treated exactly the same as any other thoughts; that is, experienced without judgment or preconceptions. Once you are drawn into analysing these experiences, you will turn them into rational concepts and, so doing, lose those truths that cannot be expressed in words.

Insight Meditation

Begin as in the last exercise, but keep your eyes open.

Allow your attention to follow your breath for a while, breathing deeply into the stomach, as though you are taking in air through the belly region itself.

After a while of following the breath, cease to do so and just sit there, relaxed but alert, being perfectly aware of your surroundings and anything that is taking place around you or outside, but without engaging your interest in it beyond observation. If noise and distractions irritate you or make you angry, observe your reaction but don't get caught up in concepts of failure or self-judgment.

Allow any thoughts and feelings to bubble up, but don't do more than observe them, and then let them go (and this includes any wonderful psychic vibes or visitations).

If you find you have followed a train of thought, bring your attention back to a quiet, noninvolved observation.

You are observing the way your body feels, your emotions, your thoughts and feelings, any noises and distractions, but you are not attaching any specific importance or attention to them; you are merely accepting them without the mind running after them. You should not be in a trance state, but totally focused on the unfolding panorama of the here and now.

Eventually, snuff the candle and get up.

To people keen to get on with visualisation, the Buddhist meditation techniques may seem a boring waste of time. However, while visualisation techniques are useful for building up our skills in ritual and magic, they are not intended to be an entertainment, and if regularly used as such they can distract us from the sacred meanings of life, which are the goal of all spiritual practices; in other words, they are not meant to be an end in themselves.

Perseverance in mindfulness and insight meditation can lead to some of the following benefits: the realisation of the interconnectedness of life; the realisation that separation and barriers are false concepts; a deep love for all other life forms; equanimity; increased energy; increased creativity; the ability to let things go.

Visualisation

Meditation centred around visualisation can be either active or passive. In other words, we can take a thought, image, or concept as our focus and see what it suggests to us—as when exploring one of the elements, or a deity—or we can deliberately build up imagery, as when learning to project energy or call in the four quarters when casting the circle. Sometimes we experience a mixture of the two.

A good way to begin a visual meditation is to mentally cast a circle of protection around yourself, though don't forget to disperse it again when you are finished. This kind of barrier will keep out any stray energies that might have been a nuisance while your chakras are open, as they will be during meditation.

Visualisation techniques are used in circle casting and in magic, so practicing them is quite an important part of witchcraft . . . though many people are naturally talented in visualisation and don't ever bother to train themselves deliberately.

One very simple way to experience visualisation is to sit in a quiet, candlelit place, breathe deeply and calmly until you have relaxed into a light trance, and then let images present themselves to you. Very often, this kind of freewheeling meditation will release important symbols from your subconscious mind, much as happens in dreams. You should pay attention to these symbols, as they may be trying to inform you in some way. At times in my life I have received important insights into my current spirituality in this way, and on occasion have seen symbols that have later come to be significant. During this type of meditation, you may also receive clairvoyant images or messages, or a sense of the presence of the Goddess and God. I remember one such occasion: I was sitting in front of a candle flame, just keeping my consciousness open and aware, when the whole room seemed to fill up with oak leaves, and I felt the presence of the God and felt his antlers as though they were growing from my own head. Another time, during May, I could see hawthorn and apple blossom behind my closed eyes, and felt a young, merry female presence.

Here are some visualisation exercises for you to try. They are only suggestions, and can be altered or replaced with others.

Crystal Visualisation

This exercise can be used to sharpen up your visualisation skills, or it can be employed to intuitively explore the qualities of a specific type of crystal or mineral.

Sit comfortably in a quiet, candlelit space, with flowers and incense.

Close your eyes.

Mentally choose a type of crystal that appeals to you.

In your mind's eye, hold the crystal in your hand, feeling its weight and texture.

Look at its colour, shape, size, surface reflections, and the way the light plays over it or strikes highlights within it.

Turn it around and examine it from every angle.

Allow your eye to be drawn into its depths, examining any flaws and striations.

Imagine that you are being drawn in deeper, until you seem to be inside the crystal itself, and see what the experience brings you.

Try to sense the energies the crystal evokes in you.

Finally, bring your concentration back out of the crystal, mentally put it to one side, and open your eyes.

You will note that I have not suggested what you should think and feel and experience. This is not a guided meditation exercise, and what you discover should be totally personal to you and in line with your current needs and perceptions.

You can repeat this exercise using another subject instead, perhaps a flower or fruit, or one of the magical tools used in the circle. You can also go deeper and try to intuit more information.

Athame Meditation

In your quiet, candlelit space, sit holding your athame in your hands.

Breathe deeply and calmly until you feel yourself entering a light trance state.

Open your awareness to the athame, letting it "speak to you."

Dwell on the concept of this being a tool of air.

Concentrate on the way the athame gathers or projects power.

Keep your mind open and receptive, and let it follow any ideas that come to you regarding the athame, its use in the magical circle, and air. Let any associated images unfold themselves.

When you sense you have explored the subject enough, come back to yourself and write about your experiences.

This meditation can be repeated with each of your magical tools if you wish.

Shaping Light

Go *to your* usual quiet meditation spot, light candles and incense, then breathe calmly for a while, closing your eyes.

Imagine that you are surrounded by shimmering light, enclosing your body, glowing all around you. What colour does it appear to you?

As you breathe in, see this light being replenished.

Breathe in and out a few times, watching the light being energised and renewed, noting how the quality of the light is affected, whether it becomes brighter or changes colour on the "in" breath.

Next time you breathe out, push light along your arms to your hands (you may feel a tingling in your palms as you do so).

See a ball of glowing light forming in the inner hollow of each hand.

With each outward breath, see the balls of light grow larger.

Push your palms toward each other and see the spheres of light merge from two smaller to one large one.

Breathe in and pull the light back into your hands, your arms, and then your aura.

Touch the ground to earth yourself, then open your eyes.

Eat.

Instead of spheres of light, you might want to experiment with visualising a stream of light, such as is used in magical work. Try changing the colour of the light, and observe whether this evokes a different emotional response, or makes you feel more or less stimulated or active.

Building an Inner Sanctuary

Sit in your candlelit space, close your eyes, and breathe deeply until you feel calm, centred, and have entered a light trance.

Turn your attention inward and begin to think about what your ideal inner sanctuary would be like. Would it be a quiet room, such as you are sitting in, or a forest glade, or maybe a circle of standing stones? It might even be a den, or tree house that you loved as a child.

When you have decided which place most appeals to you as your sanctuary (let your intuition guide you here), begin to build it up in your imagination. Try to see the surroundings as they would be; imagine any sounds, smells, textures, and so forth, that would be present. If it is outdoors, what time of year is it? Is there a breeze, sunshine, moonlight? If indoors, what is the light source, and which direction does it come from? Are there candles or a fire, or is it quite dim and calm?

Visualise a place that is comfortable and where you feel safe. Build the surroundings up bit by bit, taking your time and getting everything the way you want it. You may find that you start out with one idea, but that other images take over, perhaps taking you by surprise. If that's the case, go with the experience, as long as it is positive. Remember, this is *your* space, and anything that feels comfortable to you is okay.

You may find that your sanctuary is quite abstract, not very visual at all, maybe composed of comforting feelings, or it may be very realistic and complex, with all sorts of plants and wildlife if it's outdoors, or detailed furnishings and fabrics if indoors. Sit quietly in your sanctuary for a while, taking in the atmosphere, the details.

Let the surroundings begin to fade out, to be replaced by your everyday environment, then open your eyes, write up your experiences, and go and eat.

If you do this exercise over a period of time, you will find that your sanctuary becomes more and more real. If you find it useful to do so, you can build the image of the sanctuary when you want to go inside of yourself for meditation or peace. Some people find the inner sanctuary exercise very helpful, while others don't need it. If you are not the type of person who needs to build a realistic inner space in which to meditate, then use the exercise as an aid to practicing visualisation.

Guided Meditation

Guided meditation is much more controlled and elaborate than ordinary visualisation, though the way you interpret the material will be entirely personal. One reason I dislike this type of meditation is that it can depend too much on somebody else's idea of what you should experience. However, pathworking, which is a special kind of guided meditation based on the paths on the Tree of Life, or sometimes on tarot cards, can give valuable insights into archetypal symbols or access to established esoteric systems such as the Qaballah. If you like guided meditations, then try to devise your own as well as relying on other people's. To demonstrate guided meditation in action, and to give you a taste to see if you like the technique, here are some examples for you to consider. You might want to record them, reading them slowly, to play when you are doing the exercises, or you could read them through to get the gist and then use them as a basis. Try to carry out the exercises in a quiet place, where you will not be disturbed. You need to get comfortable, as with all meditation. Lighting candles and incense can help to create the right atmosphere. Some people like to play music as a background to the visualisations. I prefer not to do this, as music, being highly emotive, can have too great a part in shaping your mood and expectations. However, this is a matter of personal preference, and if you think music will be helpful, then use it.

When you follow the meditations, take your time, allowing yourself space to explore all the visual and tactile references, seeing what they evoke in you. Even though this type of visualisation seems so specific, my experience of group workings is that everyone has different images and emotions during a guided meditation.

Meeting the Horned God Visualisation

Start by breathing slowly and deeply, letting go of tension or stress. Close your eyes and imagine that your everyday surroundings are fading back, but that another scene is slowly forming around you.

You are in a forest clearing. It is a late afternoon in summer and you can hear birds singing. Behind you is a massive and ancient oak tree, its branches spreading wide and high above you, its leaves rich green, the foliage so dense that when you look up you can only catch glimpses of blue sky. The ridged bark is rough against your back, and leaf mould from many autumns crumbles under your feet. The oak feels so old, so strong, so timeless.

It is warm and sunny, very dry under the tree where you are sitting, but you can smell the fresh dampness of the earth, and can see raindrops sparkling on the leaves of the trees at the edge of the clearing, so you know it has recently rained. The air is alive with insects; butterflies that fly here and there across the clearing; drowsy clouds of midges; many different kinds of beetles that move industriously in the bark and among the twigs and leaves of the trees; centipedes scurrying over roots and loam. There are animals,

too: squirrels scamper over the forest floor or speed up tree
trunks, and something larger, maybe a fox or a rabbit, rus-
tles the bracken.

As you sit, a hush descends on the woodlands around you,
but the air is suddenly charged with tension, with excite-
ment. A faint drumming begins. At first you take it for your
heartbeat, then for a sudden return of the rain. But the tension builds, though whether inside or outside of you, you
cannot tell.

Your skin begins to tingle, scalp and hair acutely sensitive. The tree behind you is part of that life force, thrum-
ming with an ancient rhythm, though new as this year's
cycle. Yet all around is a deep calm that seems to breathe
from tree and earth; yet which gathers to a point of concentration like an indrawn breath or the flex of the bow before
the arrow flies.

The drumming deepens and increases and is all around,
filling the air, filling your veins, shaking the ground and the
leaves until, when it reaches a peak, a stag bursts into the
clearing, crashing through the branches and halting before
the further trees, antlers vivid and sharp against the paler
outline of the oaks. The drumbeat thuds, which you now
know as hoof beats, have stopped.

For the space of a breath the creature stands there, head
turned to you, and large, liquid eyes gazing into your face.
You thrill to some emotion beyond your understanding but as
basic and real as hunger and pain. Then the animal has gone,
forcing its way through the trees again. For a fleeting second
you think you see it poised between trunk and branch, and
for another moment still—by some trick of form or shadow—
you seem to see a man, antlers on his head; then the vision
fades, and all is still; the antlers you saw were only an illusion
it seems, created by a halo of twigs against the light, perhaps.
The birds start to sing again, the wild elation stills as though
it had never been. You are calm and alert.

You sense the forest fading away, to be replaced by your familiar everyday surroundings. Write down immediately all you have experienced, then eat and drink something to ground yourself.

Meeting the Goddess Visualisation

Take this meditation a step at a time, making careful note of colours, smells, and textures as you do so.

Light candles but not incense, then sit straight but relaxed, close your eyes, and breathe deeply, letting go of stress and tension.

Allow the room around you to grow more remote.

A scene begins to build up around you. It is night and you are standing on a hill overlooking the sea. It is very warm, and you can smell wild thyme. The full moon is throwing a path of silver across the water to a small beach below you. The gentle whisper of the waves breaking on the shore comes to you on the still air.

You turn and see a small white temple on the crest of the hill, surrounded by olive trees.

You walk toward the temple until you have reached the entrance, where you see a veil of filmy material hanging across the archway. As you push the curtain aside, you notice its colour and texture.

A few notes from a harplike instrument tremble on the air as you enter the temple, and the tang of incense teases your nostrils, evocative and sweet.

A brazier of fiery wood glows in the centre of the space, but most of the light comes from the moonbeams that flood through the doorway behind you.

There is a small table in front of you, carved of some aromatic, heavily grained wood, and a stool is set before it.

On the table you notice a chalice containing a pale golden liquid, and a pomegranate on a platter by which lies a curved silver knife.

You seat yourself at the table and take up the chalice, drinking deeply. The harplike notes sound again, and your being is flooded with the essence of the nectar you have drunk. You taste honey, wildflowers, herbs, yet there is bitterness, too, in the cup. You feel the distillation of a thousand summers, of bee and butterfly, fig and rose; the fruit of many autumns, of apple and plum and olive; the acrid tang of winter wood smoke; the freshness of wild spring irises, cyclamen, crocuses.

You swiftly slice the pomegranate in two, and the harp notes tremble on the air once more as you place a single seed in your mouth.

Immediately, your whole being is swept with the presence of the Goddess, with her gentleness, her cruelty, her laughter, her patience: with the sense of the Maiden—wild-running and free—the Mother who holds you in her arms, the Old One who gives wise counsel or lulls you to sleep. She speaks to you, deep in your heart, and only you know what she says.

Then she is gone and you are alone in the temple.

You turn and leave through the veiled entrance, making your way down the hill.

When you reach the spot you started from, you sense your everyday surroundings coming back into focus.

Pat your legs, open your eyes, then write about your experiences before eating something to make sure you are properly grounded.

You may not want to bother with writing about your meditation experiences, but it's amazing the details that quickly leave your mind, to be lost forever if you don't record them. You will probably find that some details emerge of which you were unaware when the meditation was happening.

There are other meditation techniques that are worth trying, and they include playing a drum with a steady beat, like a heartbeat, to take you into trance or aid pathworking; memorising the details of a chosen tarot card then using it as a gateway to explore the imagery it contains; burning incense and meditating on the emotions and images it evokes, with the intention of discovering more about it on a deeper level.

Meditation will reward you with greater visualisation and magical skills, a more peaceful and forgiving nature, and more energy, creativity, and spiritual insight. However, it is not an activity you can indulge in once in a while if you want to see solid results. You will need to set aside a specific time at least once or twice a week (though daily would be better), and make sure you will not be disturbed by friends, family, or the telephone. You will need to wait at least an hour after eating before commencing meditation, but make sure you eat afterward to ground yourself. If you come out of meditation, and particularly pathworking or guided meditation, feeling disoriented and ungrounded, then touch your body or the floor, pat your legs, verbalise your experiences.

Pay attention to your dreams once you have begun to practice meditation regularly, as they may become more vivid or meaningful, containing significant symbols or images. Also, try incorporating meditation into your rituals; the specific energies of the lunar phases or the festivals can enhance or accelerate your results. You might find a group meditation during a coven meeting very rewarding, leading to shared insights or increased understanding for everyone involved.

Meditation has been practiced for thousands of years across the globe, and we, with our rushed and stressful modern lives, can especially benefit from it.

CHAPTER SIX

The Moon

For witches, the moon is a symbol of the Goddess, the feminine, the mystery of deepest night and the candlelit circle. Although the Goddess is also the earth, the starlit sky, the rhythm of death and birth, and the growth cycles, to modern witches the moon is a special metaphor for the female half of the divine. But this has not always been the case in all regions of the world, and is still not so in far northern lands, where the sun is seen as a gentle, nurturing force, and the moon as cold, stark, and hard.

The lunar cycle is one of the primary markers for working magic. The moon goes from new, to waxing, to full, to waning, to dark in an ever-repeating cycle, and it takes approximately twenty-eight days to complete each round. This cycle affects many areas of life, from our moods, to the tides, to fertility and reproduction in ourselves and other species.

Even plants respond to the moon, and there are correct times for planting and harvesting different types of vegetables and other crops. For witches, the moon's cycle suggests the three major phases of the Goddess's being—Maiden, Mother, and Crone—the stages of fresh growth, fulfillment, and gradual decline. Aligning oneself with these lunar phases can bring not only positive magical results, but also a sense of emotional harmony and well-being, as well as spiritual and psychic unfoldment.

A proper understanding of the moon's cycle is essential for both magical and celebratory practice, and in the following sections I will describe the moon's phases and the type of magical work and ritual material that would be appropriate for each—though these are only suggestions and can be adapted and altered as you wish. It is the practice of my coven, and many other groups and solitaries, to call on both Goddess and God during lunar rituals; however, because the purpose of this chapter is to explain the energies of the moon itself, I have focused invocations on the Goddess alone (except for the full moon rituals). Don't let this stop you from adapting them for general use and including the God if you wish.

The New Moon

When we first enter the new moon phase, the moon itself is invisible. However, when it goes from waning/dark to dark/new, it is possible to feel the change in energy as a lift in spirits and a sense of being recharged and ready for fresh efforts. This is the start of the Maiden phase of the Goddess. Many new ideas may come to us, and this is a good time to meditate on them, examining them mentally, prior to developing them in the world of form. In symbolic terms, the Goddess is moving from a baby to a young girl to an adolescent during this phase. I use the symbolism loosely, though, for while the God dies and is reborn annually, the Goddess

does not die but simply moves through an endlessly repeat-
ing cycle that encompasses all the stages of womanhood.

When the new moon appears as a slender crescent, the
thinnest of bright silver curves, then we can begin to use it
for magical work. Sometimes at this stage you can see the
whole of the moon as a dark globe edged on the lower right
portion of its rim by the brilliance of the new moon; this is a
very potent symbol because the dark portion of the moon
can be seen as the potential promised by the fully visible
sliver. This is not a time to continue with magical projects
already begun, but rather for anything entirely new that you
want to "sow" as a seed, and nurture as the moon waxes, giving it a final "push" at the next full moon. Examples of this
might be a fresh creative idea, a new career, or the search for
a new job. There is the sense, at this time, that anything is
possible. Everything feels new and unsullied. However, if
you want to use the new moon to initiate change after a
period of stagnation, it's a good idea to work on the waning
moon to clear old conditions away first so the new has a
chance to grow unhindered.

For new moon rituals, use pure white candles and decorate the altar with pale flowers that are still in bud (symbolic
of the potential that will unfold as the moon waxes), particularly during spring and summer. Use light scented incense
such as damiana or lavender. This is the time of Artemis/
Diana the Huntress, and Aradia, and they can be invoked
now and asked to give their blessings on your work.

New Moon Invocation

O Maiden of the waxing moon,
wild lady running strong and free,
bring growth to all I choose to nurture in this moon's cycle,
to the free will of all and the harm of none,
in accordance with what is right for me.

New Moon Purification Spell

For this you will need:

- One black and one white or silver candle
- Lavender oil
- An incense that includes lavender or another light, floral scent
- A chalice of spring water or purified tap water

Casting a circle is optional, and it is preferable not to raise any energy, but you can have white candles and flowers on your altar or shrine if you wish.

You *must* do this spell on the *exact* day of the new moon, and preferably as close to the actual hour as possible—an ephemeris, magical almanac, astrological calendar, or diary will tell you when that is, though you need to make sure you have taken the time difference between your location and GMT (Greenwich Mean Time) or universal time into account, or summertime clock changes if your source gives universal or GMT for the time of the new moon (an ephemeris will, but calendars and diaries often give local clock time). If you leave it later, the moon will be properly waxing and, therefore, the purification will be less effective because energy will be increasing, and to purify you have to shed or diminish something.

If it's daylight outside, draw the curtains before lighting any altar candles and the incense.

Sit relaxed but alert, and let your breathing settle into a calm, regular pattern.

Pick up the black candle and visualise any negativity in your life being poured into it—any apathy, tiredness, ill health, sorrow, depression, and so on. See all the bad things, like a muddy stream, flowing from your hands into the wax.

Then light the candle and say, "Impurities be gone!" Blow the candle out with full force.

You can now light the candle again, putting it somewhere safe afterward to burn itself out.

Then pick up the white or silver candle and prime it with lavender oil (be warned, if you are using a silver candle, stroke the oil on very gently and sparingly or you will end up with silver paint all over your hands).

Visualise the freshness of the new moon—its pure, clear light—and see them filling your whole being, washing you clean.

Light the candle.

Lastly, drink the water from the chalice, drawing its cleansing power into your system.

You need to burn a third of the white or silver candle each day for three days. When it is gone, look at the new moon in the sky or, if it's cloudy, visualise it in your mind. Try to draw its energy into yourself, opening your whole being to the newness and cleanness of it. Give thanks to the Maiden for her gift of clarity and love.

A Spell to Initiate a Fresh Project

You will need:

- A light, fresh-smelling incense
- White candles and white budding flowers on the altar
- A bowl of earth or compost
- Seeds (sunflower seeds are ideal, as they are large enough to handle comfortably; but really, any easily grown seeds will do, and if you use something edible, like cress or alfalfa, you have the added bonus of being able to consume your "results" and take them into yourself once they have sprouted)

Light the incense and candles.

Cast a circle if you wish.

Raise energy, then call upon the Goddess as the Maiden and ask for her blessing on your work (you can use the invocation at the beginning of the "New Moon" section, or make up your own).

Sit comfortably and visualise the goal you have in mind; try to see it as you want it to be, though leave a little leeway for things to find the best way of manifesting. See your life as it will be when the new conditions come about.

When you are clear about what you are asking for, take a handful of seeds and cup them in your hands, strongly visualising your goal as you do so.

Plant the seeds, one by one, in the bowl of earth (or take pinches of tiny seeds such as cress), then either send energy through your wand or athame into the bowl, or cup the bowl in your hands and see bright light streaming into the soil from your palms. "See" the bowl filled with the green of fresh growth. Say:

As these seeds grow, may my wish become reality.
And it harm none, so mote it be.

Put the bowl of seeds in a well-lit spot until they sprout and can be planted, or, during winter, are big enough to be placed in individual pots. Seed magic is symbolic, so don't panic if your seeds don't grow for some reason . . . it doesn't mean the spell has failed.

The First Quarter Moon

As the moon waxes, it moves from the phase of the Maiden toward that of the Mother. Midway between these points the first quarter occurs, when the moon describes a half-circle in the sky, with the lit half to the right. This is a potent time magically, for energies are balanced briefly before moving forward to their peak at full moon. The feeling can best be described as peaceful expectance. We know we are moving toward the culmination of our magical efforts, we know the passion and power of the full moon is approaching, yet this is a pause when we can examine our goals and see how they are shaping. The energies of this moon's phase can best be used by meditating thoughtfully on any magic begun at the new moon, then putting a little extra force into the spell. If you are using candle magic, then spend extra time when you relight your candle, reaffirming your intentions and spending a little longer than usual visualising the realisation of whatever result you are working toward. It is a time of dynamic balance, when increase is inevitable, yet we experience a pause, an indrawn breath that is laden with potential. Think positively now, and you will steer your intentions toward a satisfactory realisation at full moon.

You can also use this time to concentrate on your relationships (including your relationship with yourself), asking for harmony and goodwill to form part of the way you interact with others. Remember that you are asking for your own part of any relationship only; you cannot steer or control the way another relates to you, but often by improving our own portion of a relationship we improve the whole.

The Full Moon

The full moon period covers three days, a day when the moon's power is reaching its maximum, the day it climaxes, and the following day during which the power is still extremely strong but is beginning to ebb away. The exact moment after the moon reaches astronomical fullness, it begins to wane. For this reason it is better to do full moon magical work before the build-up of energy peaks; in fact, if the actual full moon falls during daylight hours, then do any rituals the night before, when its power will be stronger. It is possible to use the third day of the full moon for gain—the time when the power first begins to decrease—but the results will probably not be so satisfactory or fulfilling or long lasting, although they might be.

This is the Mother phase of the Goddess, of Isis and Demeter, the pregnant, fertile phase of the moon when etheric energy is at its most abundant, and magic to obtain tangible, material results is most effective. Outside on a clear night, everything is bathed in brilliant yet muted white light. Psychic abilities are enhanced and there is a pronounced aura of mystery. Living creatures, ourselves included, seem to respond with emotional intoxication.

Traditionally, magical groups, especially witches' covens, have always met at the full moon. Any magical work involving obtaining a definite result is valid now and will almost certainly be successful on some level, but this is a particularly effective time to obtain results for goals set in motion at the new moon. It is also a period during which clairvoyant and healing abilities are heightened, and the sacred circle can be used for scrying and other forms of divination as well as joyous celebration.

Burn silver or ivory-white candles, and place fully opened flowers on the altar. Incenses to use include Isis, sandalwood, rose, coconut, lotus, and anything with a rich, full scent.

Full Moon Invocation

The moon is full and the cosmic tides are at the flood.
Beloved Lady,
Great Mother,
you who are known by many faces and many names,
bring your blessings to our work.
Make our wishes manifest in the world of form.

Goddess Invocation

Demeter, Isis, Inanna,
Queen of the heavens, Mother of all,
may your loving radiance fill our hearts,
may we open ourselves to the gifts you bring.
Let us use them with wisdom and trust,
that they may bear fruit in the world.

Magical Full Moon Rite for a Coven

Place white flowers and candles on the altar.

Set up the circle as usual, then drum, chant, or dance to raise energy.

Call on the Goddess and God to be present and ask for them to bless and empower the rite.

Sit in a circle and let each person think quietly for a while of something they want to bring into their lives. Each wish should be visualised strongly.

When everyone is ready, move clockwise round the circle, and let each person state out loud what it is they want to work magic for. As each wish is voiced, everyone should try to visualise its fulfillment as strongly as possible.

When all the wishes have been expressed, everyone should link hands, left hand under, right hand over, as this helps the energy to flow better.

Everybody should mentally begin to draw up the raised energy of the circle, seeing it as silvery white light that they begin to push to the person on their left, shaping it gradually into a cone that spins clockwise, gaining speed, rising in height.

As the cone of power gains in force, going clockwise round the circle, each person in turn should say one word that represents his or her magical wish, the words being spoken faster and faster so they become a chant.

All the while the cone of power will be building and building until, at last, one or more people will sense that it is ready to be released and will call "Now!" or will sharply break the link with the hands of the people on either side of them.

Feast.

Thank the Goddess and God and take down the circle as usual.

Magical Full Moon Rite for One

If you work alone sometimes or all the time, the above rite can be adapted. Follow the instructions for the coven rite, but instead of raising a cone of power, chant your wish over and over again, visualising the energy of your voice gaining power until it can no longer be contained, and then shooting up above your head like a spear or an arrow that will carry your desire with it.

The Waning Moon

As soon as the moon reaches full, it begins to wane, though it would be best to leave magical work involving decrease until at least two or three days after the astronomical point of fullness. Slowly but surely both psychic and physical energies begin to wind down, just as the moon's orb in the sky becomes smaller and less round. This is not a time to initiate new projects, or work any kind of magic for increase or gain, because the life force is on the ebb—in fact, it is difficult to find the incentive or enthusiasm for fresh things when the moon is waning . . . the ideas may be there but somehow we lack the necessary "push." This is more a time for banishing unwanted and negative conditions from our lives, for letting go of things that have outlived their purpose for us, and for inner, spiritual work or meditation. This is the time of the

Goddess as Wise Grandmother. We can clear the ground ready for the next waxing phase, just as gardeners clear weeds and other debris from the soil prior to planting.

For waning moon rituals, black candles are appropriate. You may want to leave your altar bare of flowers, or leave dead flowers from your last ritual, since they symbolise the forces of dissolution and decay, the breakdown of the old that clears the way for, or composts the seeds of the new, which has not yet been born.

Spell to Let Go of Outworn Conditions

This ritual is to be done during the waning moon but before the dark of moon.

You will need:

- A sombre incense, such as myrrh or patchouli
- A black candle
- A bowl of earth or compost
- Some dried, dead flowers or leaves
- Spring water and something to eat

Cast a circle, having lit the incense and the point candles but not the altar candles.

Raise energy by chanting wordlessly, rocking back and forth, and beating your hands on your thighs.

Call on the Wise Grandmother to be present. If you want you can use the following invocation:

Wise Grandmother,
understanding friend and guide,
be with me tonight.
I need your strength and compassion.
Give me the courage to open my hands,
and let fall the things that hold me back.
Like composted leaves may they nourish new growth.

As *you say* this, crumble the dead leaves or flowers into the soil.

Strongly visualise the negativity falling from you, just as the desiccated vegetation falls from your hands. Remember to be sure that your intentions are free of any thought of harm to others, no matter how much you think they may be adversely affecting you. Your job is to banish the negativity that reaches you, not the person sending it.

Now take the black candle, hold it loosely in your cupped hands, and pour all negative blocks and doubts into it, pushing them counterclockwise (or widdershins) as you do so, voicing them one by one, all the detrimental things that are surrounding various areas of your life. See the negativity spiralling into the candle until you feel you have done enough.

Light the candle, saying:

As this candle burns,
so will all negative blocks dissolve.
May fresh growth take their place when the
moon waxes again.
So mote it be. Blessed be.

Now place the candle in the bowl of earth and leaves, imagining that this will be compost to nourish new growth in your life to take the place of the old.

Plan to relight the candle every night for a period, trying to time its burning so that it has burned right down on the last day of the old moon (leave it burning overnight on the last day, if necessary). Keep the soil moist and place the bowl in a fireproof container (your cauldron would be ideal) so there is no danger of the candle setting fire to anything.

With all banishing spells, it is best to do a rite for fresh growth when the new moon arrives; by doing so, you don't leave a void, but replace the outworn with something fresh and positive. You could use your compost to grow seeds, or scatter it on the garden to feed the plants.

An alternative way to work this spell would be to project the negativity counterclockwise into the dried leaves only, then light a black candle afterward as an offering to the Wise Old Goddess.

The Last Quarter

At the midpoint of the waning cycle the last quarter moon occurs, when only the left half of the moon is visible. Again, this is a time of balance, and magically very potent. But the last quarter marks a brief period when we can pause to review the work of banishing or relinquishing, and possibly concentrate on certain factors that we may find harder to release. It is also an opportunity to find balance in our relationships, with a view to resolving difficulties and dissolving the blocks within ourselves that may be spoiling our partnerships and friendships.

The Dark Moon

Toward the end of its cycle the moon wanes to a thinner and thinner crescent, until at last it cannot be seen at all, and this period is ruled by the Hag or Crone phase of the Goddess, personified by deities such as Cerridwen and Hecate. Everything feels very calm and still, but any extra effort, either mental or physical, is likely to leave us feeling flat and drained, and it seems to take longer to accomplish ordinary tasks. However, inner work can be very potent now, as can scrying and other forms of divination of a receptive nature. It is a time of great spirituality and wisdom.

At dark moon it would be appropriate to leave the circle unlit, or light the point candles only. If you have left full moon flowers on your altar, letting them gradually degenerate as the moon wanes, then leave them now until the new moon.

Dark Moon Meditation

Although I have called this a meditation, anything that heals us or clears away blocks or benefits us in any other way via our own efforts and intent is magic.

You will need a black candle and incense similar to that used for the waning moon ritual—myrrh would be fine.

Wait until darkness has fallen. Cast a circle, but do not light any candles, and that includes the point candles, though you will need matches and your black candle near you. Don't raise any energy, as this is a quiet meditation.

Sit near the altar and gradually calm and steady your breathing.

Feel your body getting heavier and heavier until you feel as if your whole attention is sinking lower and lower and you are rooted to the floor, rooted into the earth beneath you.

Try to visualise the circle around you as a cauldron or container that enfolds you in a quiet, potent darkness where the life force is sleeping yet filled with the potential for future growth. Imagine that the cauldron is the womb of the Earth Mother, a place where leaves and root tendrils, flesh, bones, and other debris mulch down to nourish the sleeping seeds.

Now imagine that your own centre somehow coincides with the depths of the earth womb so that all is contained inside you, yet you are still cradled in the womb of the Goddess as Crone.

Listen to the stillness, draw in a breath, and hold it while you feel the enormous potency contained in this quiet, introspective time. This is the pause before the outward cycle begins again, the moment that holds the potential of all that is to come, all that could be possible when the energies flow creatively again at the imminent new moon. Value this still moment. See what it has to say to you. See how all your discarded choices and outworn patterns of being have become the loam that will feed the seeds of fresh endeavours. Sense what these new acts of creativity, of creation, will be. Lovingly and willingly let go of anything you don't need, secure in the knowledge that nothing is lost to us or wasted . . . everything lives on in another form. Breathe out and let go.

Calmly reach for your candle and matches, then light your black candle to honour the Crone and thank her for all you have experienced.

Working with all the moon's phases, not just the full moon, helps us to realize that all stages of women's lives are valid and of value, not just the times of youth and motherhood (as our society tends to imply). We should cherish the wisdom, calmness, and experience of old age equally, with the enthusiasm and energy of youth and the fruitfulness of the reproductive years. Furthermore, a thorough understanding of the lunar cycle can and should be integrated with the celebration of the solar cycle and the eight festivals, so that each year is an integrated whole, a pattern of ritual that encompasses and interweaves all the different ingredients to make a rich and rewarding fabric of spiritual existence.

CHAPTER SEVEN

The Festivals

The eight sacred seasonal festivals stretch back into antiquity, though not all eight have always been practiced simultaneously. For our remote ancestors, the year was divided in two because of the movement of herds of animals as they migrated from summer to winter pastures and back again, followed by the humans who first hunted, and later domesticated them. The Great Mother, the Goddess, who nurtured all in her womb through both life and death, was wooed in turn by the Holly King, Lord of Winter, and the Oak King, Lord of Summer, who fought at the turning points of the seasons, the Oak King dying at midsummer to be reborn into power at midwinter, in turn defeating the Holly King once more.

Later, as people settled and began to farm the land, the two Gods became one, the dying and resurrecting vegetation god who is born at Yule and matures with the unfolding seasons, mating with the Goddess in the spring, then dying with the harvest, to be reborn once more the following Yule.

In present times, the two annual themes have become intertwined so that we celebrate both cycles, and can no longer separate the strands of myth. There are four solar festivals, the Winter and Summer Solstices and Spring and Autumn Equinoxes, and four fire festivals, Imbolc, Beltane, Lammas, and Samhain, which have come down to us from Celtic times. Each festival has its own symbolism and decorations. For the four solar festivals, a sunwheel can be made by tying a circle of some pliable, thin branches like willow and reinforcing it with a cross in the centre—the wheel of the sun quartered by the four solar rites—and this can be decorated with seasonal flowers and hung in the house, or a tree outside, or propped against the altar. For other festivals, seasonal flowers and fruits are brought in and placed on the altar or around the home.

For modern-day pagans, the eight festivals are a way of tuning into the seasonal cycle and celebrating the meaning of Goddess and God in our lives, and of aligning both emotional and spiritual development with the deeper meaning behind the turning seasons. But, really, everybody could benefit from following the Wheel of the Year, since we have become so detached from the rhythm of the seasons in the way we now live. To synchronise outer and inner activity, material and spiritual, to follow the ebb and flow and cadence of the year's pulse can bring contentment, stability, and joy into our lives, the satisfaction of knowing that we are following the natural order rather than a false pattern imposed by manipulating the seasons to suit our greed for overproduction.

The following are a set of seasonal rituals, all of which have been used by myself or the coven I work with, though

The Wheel of the Year

they are a fairly basic framework that can be expanded and embellished, or altered from year to year if wished. They are written for people living in Britain or Europe, but they can be adapted for different climates with a little forethought and planning. If you are unable to obtain, or don't like some of my ingredients, or the place where you live has different fruits, flowers, and so forth at the festival times, then please, please feel free to adapt and improvise. Witchcraft is a creative and flexible religion, and as long as you stick to the essence of each seasonal rite, then interpret in whatever way suits you.

All the rituals were written for a group, but all can be used by one person or a couple with little alteration.

Yule or Winter Solstice: December 21

Throughout the world and down through the centuries, Yule, or the Winter Solstice, has always been the most sacred and magical of the festivals. It is the one that has been the least eroded by the passage of time, and this is partly because of its adoption by Christianity to be the birth time of Jesus, though, in fact, most of the eight festivals have been adapted by the Christian calendar and appear as Christmas, Candlemass, Easter, Saint John's Day, Harvest Festival, and All Saints Day.

We can trace the Winter Solstice back through the ages: through Victorian Christmases with their huge, candle covered pine trees and rich food; back through the starkness of Puritan times, when its celebrations all but disappeared; through the castles and manors and hovels of medieval times, when every dwelling and place of worship was decked with ivy and holly and great swathes of fragrant pine branches— the sacred winter greenery—and feasts of precious foodstuffs were prepared; back even further through the Saxon halls, the villages of the Celts, and still further to our Neolithic ancestors, whose passage barrows allowed the rays of the rising sun to shine into the depths of the earth at the solstice, beautifully symbolising the rebirth of the light from the winter soil.

Yule is a time of immense peace and joy, when the sun's light is reborn during the greatest dark and cold, a time when peoples of old struggled to feed themselves and survive frost and snow and ice, especially on the edges of the vast forests and pine woods of ancient Europe, where food and fuel were scarce at this season and wild animals might take the surviving livestock. For them, the re-emergence of light and energy—no matter how subtle—would have been an occasion for rejoicing, a respite amid the winter gloom when they could eat and drink their fill, secure in the knowledge that the sun's power would wax from now on through to spring and the return of easier times.

At Yule, the Oak King, ruler of the waxing half of the year, defeats the Holly King, lord of the waning half of the year, and the Child of Promise is born again to bring ever-increasing light and warmth into our lives, the pledge that spring and summer will be with us once more if we are patient and wait out the barren months. This is the rebirth of the God from the womb of the Goddess—he who will grow into the Lord of the Greenwood, the great Horned One, and who is also the Sun King. We decorate our homes with ivy for the Goddess, holly for the Holly King, and mistletoe for the reborn sun.

Witches carry on the ancient traditions at Yule, decorating their homes with the sacred greenery, lighting the Yule log on the day of the solstice, feasting and exchanging gifts, though we may have a separate session at the actual solstice where we give and receive gifts with pagan friends, maintaining the tradition of exchanging presents with our families. We also have our Yule rite on the eve of the solstice, when we celebrate the miracle of the sun's rebirth, the light coming out of the earth, the renewal of creative energies.

Yule Rite

The following ritual was written for a coven, but it can be adapted for use by a couple or a solitary witch.

You will need:

- A cauldron or other container for the centre of the circle, which should be filled with dampened earth and decorated round the edge with holly, ivy, and mistletoe
- A large white candle, which should be pushed firmly into the earth in the middle of the cauldron
- A smaller white candle for each person present
- Yule incense, either bought or made at home using frankincense, myrrh, and mixed spices as part of the ingredients

- A drum (if you don't have an actual drum, then improvise)
- Seasonal food for the feast and spiced grape juice or wine for the chalice
- If you have made a sunwheel, decorate it with holly and ivy and hang it at the edge of the circle, or prop it against the altar
- On the altar itself you need your usual magical tools and altar candles, but you can also bring in sprays of evergreen oak and birch twigs (leafless at this season), for birch is the tree of rebirth, and belongs to the solstice

Light the point candles, the altar candles, and the charcoal for incense.

Ground and centre, then cast the circle and call in the quarters as usual, but don't raise energy at this point in the ritual.

If you are doing this rite with a group, then you will have to decide in advance to whom each of the ritual tasks is to be allocated. (Obviously, solitary practitioners will have to do everything themselves.) One person needs to sit near the cauldron with matches or a lighter at hand.

Extinguish all the candles. Everyone should now sit in a circle, and one person should begin a slow, steady, but quiet drumbeat, like a heartbeat.

Over the top of this, someone should speak the following invocation (this will need to have been learned beforehand because there will be no candlelight by which to read):

Under stone, under bone,
into the earth, await rebirth,
into the tomb, into the womb,
in darkness hold, still and cold . . .

The drumbeat should now cease, and everyone should fall into silent meditation, imagining themselves going deep into the cold, dark winter earth.

After a suitable time, the drumming should begin again, slowly but lightly at first.

Then someone should light the white candle in the cauldron to represent the sun being reborn from the womb of the earth, and the invocation continues with:

A point of light!

The drumming should increase at this moment, though still not too loud, as the invocation continues:

**The Child of Promise comes to us
out of the tomb, out of the womb.
The candle burns, the light returns!**

The drumming should become louder, faster, and wilder as the altar and point candles are relit, until a crescendo is reached as each person in turn lights their personal candle from the cauldron candle, then pushes it into the soil around the cauldron candle.

Now everyone can voice any ideas they want to begin to formulate for the year ahead, absent healing or other work can be done, or the energy of the circle can simply be used to send peace and love out into the world to do its healing work wherever it may be needed. If working in a group, shape the energy into a cone of power, spin it, and send it on its way. If alone, direct it with the mind or a wand or athame.

It only remains to consecrate cakes and wine, and feast, before taking down the circle.

Imbolc: February 1

Little by little the waxing light of the sun increases until, by the beginning of February, the days are noticeably longer. There may have been recent snow or rain, and it is still very cold, but the first hints of spring are beginning to appear as buds form on twig and branch, celandine, snowdrops, and crocuses push up through the frosty soil, and the first lambs are born out in the fields.

Imbolc is one of the Celtic fire festivals, celebrated by the lighting of candles in acknowledgment of the sun's increasing power, the reawakening of energy from within the land. It is also a time of purification, symbolising the washing away of winter leaves and decay so that the first green shoots can make their way into the light. The Corn Bride comes forth from the burial mounds seeking her mate, the Goddess is restored to youth after the birth of the God, and the young God himself grows toward youth and manhood, in readiness for the spring fertility rites. Brighid, a solar goddess, presides over this festival, bringing her gentle, fiery energy to empower our newly formed wishes and goals. This is a time of peace and hope, when creativity begins to gather power once more, symbolised by Brighid's three talents of poetry, healing, and smithcraft.

Imbolc Rite

You will need:

- Snowdrops on the altar
- A water-filled cauldron with snowdrops and white floating candles
- A small bowl of earth with a fresh white candle in it, placed near the snowdrops on the altar (this candle represents the light and energy that germinates the first seeds in the soil)
- A plain white candle for each person present (this will be a wish candle)

- A bowl, cauldron, or other fireproof container filled with damp soil or sand in which to place the lighted wish candles
- A taper
- Imbolc incense or an incense with a light, fresh, and slightly flowery fragrance
- Spring water for the chalice and some white or milky food for the feast, as dairy foods are traditionally eaten now

Cast the circle as usual, but don't light the point candles and altar candles, only the candle in the bowl of soil, and the incense. The idea is to create the womb of the earth, in the centre of which the light burns, so no candles are needed at the periphery of the circle.

Drum to raise energy. If you own a bodhran, the traditional Celtic hand drum, then all the better, as this is sacred to Imbolc and to Brighid.

Call on Brighid to be present:

**Lady Brighid, be here with us for your
festival of fire and water.
Let us be cleansed of all we wish to leave behind,
as the earth is washed clean by the rains,
ready to bring forth new growth
under the waxing fire of the sun.**

Everybody should sit in a circle and, going round the circle in turn, say what they feel they need to let go of.

When this is done, the taper should be lit from the single white candle, then touched to the floating candles until the water-filled cauldron is glowing with soft light. This cauldron of fire and water and floating snowdrops represents the purifying essence of Brighid, and it will cleanse all present so they can turn to fresh projects.

Now each person should pick up their white wish candle and, formulating a new wish or goal to work on through the year, hold the candle to their third eye and strongly visualise their wish.

Each person should light their candle from the main candle in the earth-filled bowl, saying:

May Brighid empower my wish,
as she germinates the spring seeds.

Consecrate the chalice of spring water; as each person drinks in turn, they should feel the purifying effect of the water flushing through their system, cleansing and energising.

Continue with the feast and then end the circle, thanking the Goddess for her presence by saying:

We thank you, Lady, and bid you farewell.

The wish candles should be put somewhere safe to burn down. Any soil that has contained Imbolc candles can be kept until Oestara, at which time you can plant seeds in the soil if you want. You might also like to keep some of the water from the cauldron to use in the next moon rite that you do. It will retain the wonderful fresh, gentle essence of Imbolc.

Corn Bride Rite

This simple ritual has been adapted from the traditional Imbolc custom of putting out the lights in a community and waiting for a chosen maiden to bring a lighted rush taper from house to house to rekindle the light of spring. It can be performed within circle, or can be part of an open gathering or family celebration, and is especially successful if children take part and bring in the flame. If only adults are participating, then one woman should represent the maiden who brings in the light. I will describe it as though it is intended for an open gathering of friends and their families in someone's house.

You will need:

- A white candle for each light carrier
- A white candle for each participant
- A large earth- or sand-filled container in which to place the lit candles
- Greenery and snowdrops to make crowns for each light bearer; you may want to make wire crowns into which to weave the greenery
- Snowdrops for decoration
- A corn dolly (make one from wheat or other grain on the stem if you don't have one; you will need a bunch for the main body and one for the arms, and twine to tie them together and to twist round the top quarter to form a head)
- A pine cone or a traditional pine cone-tipped or acorn-tipped phallic wand to represent the God
- Milk, cheese, and other dairy foods to form part of the feast

The corn dolly should be dressed in white to become the Corn Bride (a doll's dress or clean new lacy white handkerchief would do), then laid in a small basket or other wicker or rush container with the pine cone or phallic wand by her side.

The table should be decorated with snowdrops and the food, with the Corn Bride lying in the centre.

Everybody except the light bearer(s) should sit in one room, and the lights should be put out.

The light bearer(s), wearing their crowns, should come in from another room, bearing their lit candles, and everyone should light their own candles from these (please remember to closely supervise small children when they are carrying candles). As each person kindles their candle, they should say:

The candles can be pushed into the bowl of earth and left to
burn throughout the following feasting.

Oestara/Spring Equinox: March 21

Throughout the weeks from Imbolc, light and warmth gain
in strength until, by the solar festival of Oestara, the hours
of night and day are equally balanced. Nature is rioting with
growth, the tender leaves of spring unfurling on twig and
branch; the banks are carpeted with primroses and violets,
daffodils nod and dance, and birds are nesting amid the first
delicate blossoms in the hedgerows. In the fields and at the
eaves of the greenwood, the rampant young Stag God pur-
sues the Maiden of Flowers, their teasing courtship dance
setting the forest aflame with verdant fire.

This is the time of rebirth, when the light will soon outstrip
the darkness and the sun will grow in power each day. The
nights can still be frosty, but the days are quite warm in shel-
tered places out of the brisk spring breezes, though short,
sharp showers of heavy rain can soak the grass and send baby
rabbits scampering for the shelter of their burrows. It is the
seeding time, and seed magic is very appropriate for Oestara . .
. the planting of seeds represents the goals we began to express
at Yule and germinated with our wish candles at Imbolc.

Witches and pagans continue the ancient tradition of
painting designs on eggs to celebrate this renaissance of
energy and warmth, the upsurge of fertility. There are
chocolate Easter eggs, too, along with Easter bunnies and
fluffy yellow chicks. This is the official beginning of spring.

Oestara Rite

At this festival, it is wonderful to fill the whole ritual space
with masses of daffodils, primroses, forsythia, and other sea-

sonal flowers, and to light the whole perimeter of the circle, between the point candles, with coloured candles . . . though leave enough space to move freely without risk of catching swirling robes or clothing alight. You can also decorate a sunwheel with daffodils and other spring flowers, and bring it into the circle if you like.

You will need:

- Spring flowers
- Decorated eggs for the altar (optional)
- Candles in pastel shades of green, pink, yellow, and mauve
- One black and one white candle to be placed in holders on the altar in front of the usual altar candles
- Seeds
- A bowl of earth, possibly one used at Imbolc
- Oestara incense, or something with a fresh, flowery scent
- Hot cross buns, simnel cake, or other cakes decorated for the Oestara theme for the feast
- Spring water, juice, or wine for the chalice

Light the incense, altar candles, point candles and any decorative candles, and the black candle, but leave the white candle unlit.

Cast the circle, and raise energy by drumming, dancing, or chanting.

Then call on the Goddess and God to be present:

**O Lady of Flowers,
Lord of the Springtime Woods,
bring light and life and growth to our rite
and into our lives.
Hail and welcome!**

Now one person should light the white candle from the black one to represent the light half of the year taking power from the dark half, saying:

We welcome the waxing light.

Then put the black candle out, leaving the white one to burn until the end of the ritual; it can be lit on successive evenings until it is burned down, thus lighting the path of spring.

All present should now sit in a circle and take a seed, cupping it in their hands and empowering it with energy as they visualise the goal that they first began to work on at Imbolc, and which is now ready to be planted.

When everyone is finished, the bowl of earth should be passed round the circle so that the seeds can be pushed into the soil.

Now each person in turn can hold the bowl in cupped hands and channel energy into it, or direct a stream of energy with wand or athame, or else a cone of power can be raised and directed downward into the bowl rather than being spun higher and released.

Feast, then thank the Goddess and God for their presence:

**Horned Lord whose green fire quickens the seeds,
Gentle Lady in whose womb they grow,
we thank you for your gift of
freshness and inspiration.
Hail and farewell.**

Now, open the circle as usual.

The old Celtic fire festival of Beltane brings in summer amid an abundance of fragrant blossom: apple, hawthorn, and pear. Under the spreading branches of oak and birch, where newborn deer lie in the dappled light and the cuckoo calls, the floor of the woods is hazy with the heavenly azure of bluebells. The meadows' lush grass is speckled with daisies and buttercups, and cattle graze sleek-flanked. In city parks and gardens, the chestnut candles glow, and lilacs spread their sweetness into the warm, milky air. Beltane's shout of joy echoes throughout the whole month of May.

In times gone by, young men and women spent the last night of April in the woods, enacting the greenwood marriage in honour of the Goddess and God, who—as the Maiden of Flowers and the Lord of the Greenwood—fulfill the Sacred Marriage every May Eve. On May Morning, people would bring in the May, the hawthorn blossom, the Goddess's bridal garland. Then, in every village and the separate districts of the towns, folk would dance round the maypole, weaving in and out of the twining ribbons, performing the dance of life and fertility around the phallic shaft of the pole.

Even in modern times, we still crown the May Queen (representative of the Goddess), dance round the maypole, and watch Morris Dancers and the leafy Jack in the Green—the Green Man. We witches and pagans still jump over the Beltane Bonfire to rid ourselves of the unwanted blocks and obstacles we want to discard, just as our Celtic ancestors—and farmers of later times—drove their cattle between the fires so that the smoke and heat might cleanse them of parasites and the last traces of winter disease.

Beltane Rite

This ritual should be performed on May Eve, if possible. If you have an undisturbed place where you can practice rituals outdoors, especially in the woods, then that would be ideal, but it can also be done inside.

You will need:

- Hawthorn blossom
- Some sprays of oak leaves
- Other spring flowers
- A cauldron or other container filled with water, in which are apple blossom and floating candles in shades of deep pink, blue, and green
- Green and orange candles
- Benzoin or Beltane incense
- A chalice and a wand or athame
- Honeyed apple juice or mead
- Some sort of cake or biscuits for the feast

Place the hawthorn in a vase on the altar.

Place the green and orange candles around the perimeter of the circle, then light them, as well as the altar and point candles and incense.

Strew the edge of the circle with the oak leaves and spring flowers.

Light the floating candles in the cauldron.

Cast the circle, then raise energy.

Call on the Goddess and God with the invocations below:

Lady of Flowers, Summer Bride,
grace our circle with your gentle, joyful presence.
Nurture our wishes, even as you nurture
the child who grows in your womb.
Welcome, Lady, welcome.

Lord of the Greenwood, Hawk of May,
swift-moving stag,
enfold us in your gentle, fierce embrace;
father, brother, healer, lover, friend . . .

Now everybody should take it in turns to leap over the cauldron of candles and apple blossom, shouting out something they want to lose from their lives as they do so (for example: depression, irritability, tiredness).

Then all should leap back the other way and call out a wish. This is a wonderful time to reinforce the Imbolc wish, as there is a surge of power at Beltane that can carry our projects through into summer, just as crops tended well at this time could reward our ancestors with a good harvest. If you are holding this rite indoors and, like us, your floorboards don't allow too much vigorous jumping, then hop or step over the candle fire instead (holding clothing well out of the way of the flames, of course!).

At the end of jumping the "Beltane Bonfire," a chosen couple should now symbolically enact the sacred mating of Goddess and God. The woman holds up the chalice of juice or mead, and the man lowers the wand or athame into it (obviously, single-sex groups will need to adapt the material here).

Another coven member says:

> **Sacred is the mating of our Lady and Lord.**
> **From their union the young God is formed,**
> **and everything prospers.**
> **Let this abundance touch our lives,**
> **that our goals may flourish, too.**

The chalice is passed round the circle with the words "Blessed be," then it is time to feast, thank the Goddess and God, and open the circle.

You can thank the deities very simply, or use the following invocation:

> **We give thanks to the Lady and the Lord for blessing**
> **our work, and bid them farewell.**

On May Morning itself, you can build a proper bonfire out-side and repeat the fire leaping. It is also possible to con-struct a small maypole with a piece of dowelling and coloured ribbons, and sink it into the ground. The idea is for one set of people to dance clockwise, and the other counter-clockwise. As one set dances inward, the other dances out-ward. Don't worry if you don't really know what you are doing . . . we don't either, and we still manage to have fun every May Day. As the dancers weave in and out of each other, so the ribbons crisscross down the shaft of the may-pole in a rainbow tracery of colours. When the ribbons are all taken up, the dancers should reverse direction so that it all unwinds again . . . thus we enact the energies of life that flow in and out of manifestation.

May Morning is a time for celebration, for eating and drinking and merrymaking, expressing the joy of this season.

Summer Solstice: June 21

The long, hot days of June wind toward the longest day, when the sun moves into the astrological sign of Cancer for the cli-max of his power—sun and moon unite because the sun peaks in Cancer, the sign of the moon. The marriage of Goddess and God brings fruitfulness to the land. Although the bright colours of spring have dulled and deepened, crops are ripen-ing, the freshly cut hay lies drying in the sun, and the flanks of livestock swell with imminent birth. In the meadows, and on the grassy uplands where the lark sings, bees raid yellow, pink, and bronze wildflowers, and butterflies flitter languidly or drowse in the sun. And there are roses everywhere, in gardens and public parks and out in the roadside hedges.

Although the Oak King is approaching the culmination of his power, soon he will be defeated by his twin, the Holly King. The Sun King's strength is about to wane toward har-vest and autumn, and the return of life and light into the

soil. In olden times, beacons were lit on hilltops throughout
Britain on the day of the solstice to celebrate this solar festival, the zenith of the sun's supremacy.

For now, winter still seems a long way off, but we are at a
significant turning point in the year's cycle. It is not quite
time to reap our personal harvest, just as the corn is not yet
fully ripe, but we should redouble our efforts at this moment,
should charge our magical goals with fiery solar strength so
that they prosper . . . for summer will not last forever, and
from now on the sun's power will start to decrease.

Midsummer Rite

If possible, do this ritual outside. You will need:

- Roses
- Oak leaves
- Sunflowers, marigolds, honeysuckle, and other summer
  flowers
- A gold candle
- A candle in deep rose pink
- Frankincense and censer
- The usual altar trappings and ritual equipment
- A golden-coloured drink for the chalice, such as white
  grape juice, apple juice, or white wine or mead
- Biscuits, such as oat cookies, or cakes made with honey

On the altar, place roses for the Goddess and oak leaves for
the God.

Strew oak leaves and summer flowers round the circle's
perimeter.

If you have a sunwheel, then decorate it with a sunflower
head in the middle and summer flowers around the rim.
You can weave flowers into your hair as well if you wish,
or make wire crowns to decorate with flowers.

Light incense and candles and cast the circle, then drum and dance and sing to raise energy.

Light the rose pink candle with the following invocation:

Hail to the Goddess,
Great Mother of all,
lady of river and ocean and hill,
honey bee, butterfly, salmon, and eel,
the cattle in the meadow, the bird on the wing,
the swelling fruit on the bough.

Then light the gold candle and say:

Hail to the Sun,
hail to the Lord,
King of the forest, life force in the grain,
Lord of the wildwood, of squirrels, and deer,
of serpent and eagle,
we honour you now.

Each person should turn their attention to any magical goals that need reinforcing, for this is the final burst of energy before the long waiting time until harvest; so everyone should link hands and concentrate energy into the combined wishes of the group. Then any further magical or healing work can be done if so desired.

Finally, hold up the chalice and imagine the rays of the sun pouring into its contents (even if it is nighttime), then pass it round, each person taking a drink and saying:

Flower in me, fruit in me.

Similarly, bless the food and pass it around, with each person breaking off a piece and saying:

Ripen my harvest.

Now bid the Goddess and God farewell with the following
invocation:

We give thanks for abundance.
Farewell to the Lady and Lord.

Now end the rite in the usual way.

Lammas: August 1

The hot, dry days and balmy nights seem to stretch out
interminably, punctuated by fierce summer storms that only
briefly cool the air. At last, harvest arrives and the corn is
cut, and John Barleycorn is slain. The Goddess herself, in
her ageing Crone aspect, wields the sickle that sunders the
life force from the God . . . the age-old sacrifice of the grain.
The poppies at the fields' edge symbolise his blood that seeps
into the ground, the life force returning to the soil to await
its re-emergence at spring. Even the full moon around this
time of year is often blood red when it rises, reminding us
that for life to be sustained, something must die.

Lammas, or first harvest, is the time when the Corn
Mother moves toward the burial mounds, where, as the Hag
of Winter, she will wait out the time until Imbolc, when she
can come forth rejuvenated. Her Lord is slain, yet he will be
reborn at Yule; though until then he will rule the Underworld, the Land of the Dead. Because this is one of the
Celtic fire festivals, it is another time when bonfires once
blazed throughout the land.

This is also Lughnasadh, the festival of the Celtic god
Lugh, Lord of Light, and in the gardens and allotments,
huge yellow sunflowers with rich brown hearts bloom as
though in his honour. But only the cereal crops are gathered
now; apples and pears, plums and marrows are still ripening
and won't be ready for another month or so. Our own goals

may be ready to garner now, or we may need to wait till the Autumn Equinox to allow them extra time.

Lammas Rite

If this rite can be done outdoors, then so much the better; however, if you want to hold it in a corn field, choose one that has already been cut so you don't trample the crop.

Keep the whole ritual very low key and solemn.

You will need:

- Some ears of wheat, oats, or barley
- Deep golden-orange candles for the altar
- Red grape juice or wine for the chalice
- Some fresh bread for the feast (a loaf coated with poppy seeds would be ideal)
- Red poppies or sunflowers for the altar (if you want to use poppies, then cut them just before the rite, otherwise they will have wilted)
- Lammas incense or incense containing marigold petals, a few chamomile flower heads, sandalwood, sage, and a little frankincense and myrrh

Cast the circle as usual, lighting point and altar candles.

Raise energy by silently dancing in a circle, hands linked.

Call on the God:

> **Father of the grain,**
> **Spirit of the corn,**
> **you who die to feed us,**
> **We thank you for your act of selfless giving.**
> **May your fires burn one last time before you go.**

One person should now light the orange candles while someone else scatters ears of corn across the ritual space.

Now the Goddess should be invoked with the following words:

You who were the Great Mother of old,
we honour your sacrifice.
We give thanks for our personal harvest,
and we offer up our own sacrifice,
for we must relinquish all that has
failed in our own lives,
even though we know that letting go
of cherished dreams is hard.

Standing with linked hands, the group should take it in turns to list the goals that have come to fruition this harvest time, going clockwise round the group.

Then state the failed projects that need to be released (the sacrifices), as each person consciously lets go of them.

The chalice of red juice or wine should now be raised silently in tribute to the God. This is his blood (a symbolism that predates the Christian communion by many thousands of years). Then some liquid should be spilled on the ground and the ears of grain, before the chalice is passed round as usual.

Raise the loaf in the same way, to honour the Goddess who has given us the body of her lover/son that we might eat.

Pass the loaf round the circle, everyone tearing off a piece and giving silent thanks before eating.

The act of consuming bread and juice/wine takes the place of the usual thanks and farewell to Goddess and God.

End the ritual and open the circle in the usual way.

Autumn Equinox: September 21

Many fields are ploughed, the earth laid in rich, crumbling red-brown seams where white gulls wheel in search of worms and other food. The hedgerows blaze with scarlet, crimson, and russet, where rose hips, hawthorn berries, and hazelnuts flaunt their gaudy colours, and purple blackberries nestle among their own prickly foliage. The leaves are just beginning to turn, their edges splotched with yellow, rose, and pale green. Under the woodland trees, mushrooms and toadstools flourish, and beech masts crunch underfoot, scattering their triangular seeds.

There is a sadness, a stillness as the life force takes a definite inward turn. The Goddess is the earth womb that receives the fallen seeds; the God returns briefly from the underworld to fetch his mate, and there she will wait until spring comes and the life forces are renewed. Yet this is also a mellow time, when fruit trees yield their crop, and the gardens are alight with purple michaelmas daisies, bright fluorescent dahlias, and chrysanthemums in shades of bronze and gold, lavender and peach. Spiders spin their webs from bush to bush along the lanes and roadsides, and squirrels root for food to make up their winter stores. The nights may be colder now, but the days are often as warm as August, though the sun is lower in the sky and has lost his fierce bite. The mornings are wreathed in mist, the afternoons sometimes blue with smoke as the garden rubbish begins to be burned. The swallows are leaving gradually, and geese fly in skeins across the sky.

This is the time of the second harvest, the solar festival of Mabon, when the fruit crops can be picked along with runner beans, marrows, and many root vegetables. At this time of year our ancestors would have begun to store apples, turnips, and other durable food in preparation for the long, cold winter months. This is also the time of our spiritual second harvest, the reaping of those things that needed a little longer to mature. Anything that has failed entirely must be abandoned or else set aside to be worked on next year. Meanwhile, we turn our attentions inward—just as the light turns back into the dark earth—beginning the task of sorting through our subconscious blocks and motivations, the

things that drive us or hold us back. At the Autumn
Equinox, day and night are again equal, a time of balance
and harmony, but this time the nights will soon start to
lengthen. This inward turn, the swing from light to dark,
often upsets people until they adjust . . . the Autumn
Equinox falls just in Libra, and the scales seesaw wildly until
a point of equilibrium is found.

Autumn Equinox Rite

You will need:

- Apples or other autumn fruits for the altar or to be placed in a cauldron
- Autumn flowers to decorate the circle
- One white and one black candle
- An incense that contains a hint of myrrh, geranium oil, and patchouli
- Autumn fruits and bread, or fruitcake for the feast
- Juice or wine

Cast the circle.

Light the white candle to represent the light half of the year, but leave the black one unlit for now.

Drum to raise energy.

Call on the Goddess and God with the following invocation:

O Lady of the autumn woodlands,
Earth Mother, Crone, keeper of the seeds,
womb of being,
Lord of the Otherworld, Guardian of the Gates,
friend and healer,
bring harmony and fruitfulness into our circle.
We give thanks for our harvest,
for food and shelter,
strength, warmth, and friendship.

Light the black candle from the white one, to represent the dark season taking light from summer, while saying, "We welcome the dark." Then put the white candle out, but leave the black one burning till the end of the rite (it can be burned on successive evenings to light our first steps toward winter).

Now everyone should link hands and dance or whirl clockwise, shouting out the goals each person has realised at this festival. Start individually, but let the words build into a chant, one key word to represent each goal, until the whole thing is a continuous sound.

Then spin counterclockwise to voice the things each person wishes to let go of.

Finally, dance clockwise again and verbally affirm the spiritual or psychological issues you want to work on during the winter months, the time of introspection.

Bless the food and chalice with the following words:

Lord of the vine, Lady of fruit and seeds,
we give thanks for your bounty.
Blessed be.

Pass round the chalice and food.

End the rite.

Samhain: October 31 to November 1

Samhain is the Feast of the Dead, the Celtic fire festival when the gateway between our earthly plane of being and the spiritual realms is opened for a while to allow the living to commune with their dead families and friends. Not just humans traverse the causeway between one world and another, but also beloved pets. The God is the Guardian who allows the dead to travel between the different levels of being. He is the Lord of Life and Death in his Death aspect, the one some of us dread, and yet whose compassion ends suffering when the body can no longer be healed.

This is Halloween, a period when ordinary clock time holds no sway, when our paranormal powers are sharpened and we really do seem to have one foot in the Otherworld.

Outside, the wild winds have hurled all but the most stubborn leaves to the muddy ground. The trees and bushes are revealed in all the skeletal starkness of bare branch and trunk, though the first knobbly swellings at the ends of twigs show where the spring greenery will unfold. Rivers run engorged through desolate banks, and the streams are slowed by the delicate tracery of ice as frost breathes across the landscape. Nights are long and days are short now.

Against this backdrop of bleakness and cold, bonfires burn and fireworks explode into the sky. In warm houses, witches and pagans light pumpkin lanterns, bake pumpkin or apple pies, put out food, and prepare to welcome the dead. This is the time to let go, finally, of any lingering issues that cannot be resolved.

Samhain Rite

You will need:

- A cauldron or other large container filled with water and floating apples (the Celtic fruit of the dead) to be placed in the centre of the circle
- If you have or can procure one, a ram's or stag's skull (preferably a skull of a ram or stag who died a natural death!) to place on the altar to represent the God
- Small pumpkin or turnip lanterns to light the edge of the circle
- Photographs or other mementos of the dead, to be placed on the altar

- Chrysanthemums (the flowers of the dead) to go on the altar
- A candle for each person or pet to be remembered, to be left on the altar for now
- Candle holders or a sand-filled container
- A drum
- A crystal ball, witches' mirror, tarot cards, or other tools of divination
- Samhain incense, or an incense with strong overtones of myrrh and patchouli
- Pumpkin bread or spicy fruitcake, pie, and other food—there should be enough for everyone present, plus a portion for each of the individuals who are to be remembered
- Spiced fruit punch for the chalice (with or without alcohol)

Light the point and altar candles and lanterns, but not the personal candles.

Cast the circle.

One person, beating the drum with a slow, heavy beat, should lead everyone round the circle, spiralling counterclockwise toward the centre (if you are doing this ritual in a fairly small room, you will have to stop before everyone reaches the centre).

The Goddess and God are invoked as follows:

> **Dark Goddess of winter, Wise One, Hag,**
> **tonight we stand on the threshold of the**
> **Celtic New Year,**
> **the time that is no time,**
> **and the Gateway between the worlds stands wide.**
> **Come forth, come forth, O Lord of Life and Death,**
> **guard the gate through which our loved ones pass.**
> **Those who have died and those yet unborn,**

They are one and the same.
Welcome, welcome, welcome,
those who have come to share this time with us.
There is no death but only change!

The person at the outer end of the spiral line should now lead everyone out again and into a normal circle.

Everyone should now be seated round the cauldron.

Each person should take one candle to light for each loved one they wish to honour, and should light the candles, saying who they are remembering, and telling a little about the individual's life and why they are missed.

Push the candles into the sand-filled container.

One member of the group should say:

Dear ones who have walked
the space between the worlds
to be with us tonight,
we welcome you with love and joy.

Bless the food and drink with the following invocation:

Horned One, Lord of the Underworld,
friend, guide, and comforter,
may this feast be consecrated in your name
and that of the Lady.
Let our dear ones stay for a while
and eat and drink with us
before they return to your realm of rest and peace.

Send the chalice and food round the circle, putting out portions of food for the unseen guests.

When everybody has eaten as much as they want, let there be a space of silent communion with the dead, or of meditation on the meaning of death, the afterlife, and rebirth.

Pass round the scrying tools or tarot cards and let anyone who wishes use them. Some people might want to scry in the water in the cauldron.

Close the circle down with the following invocation:

Wise Lady, stern Lord,
we thank you for your presence,
and we bid farewell to both you and our beloved dead.
One day we will be reunited beyond the veil of Death,
or in the world of form.
Until then we give thanks for the time
we have spent together tonight.
Farewell.

End the rite in the usual manner.

Samhain Celebration for Family or Friends

This is a nonritualistic way to celebrate Samhain, and children can join in. You will need:

- A candle for each individual to be remembered (we have found Hanukkah candles or small birthday candles to be very effective)
- A cauldron or other fireproof container filled with sand
- A photograph or other memento, or the name of each individual written on paper
- Pumpkin and turnip lanterns to decorate the room
- Apples
- Food including pumpkin soup, pie, and so on
- Tarot cards, scrying tools, and the like
- Musical instruments and/or poetry and prose appropriate to the season and the theme of the festival, to read aloud
- Halloween costumes for any children, if wished

Light a candle for each individual to be remembered, then push it into the sand-filled container.

Place the name, photo, a poem, or other memento against the container of candles.

When all are done, welcome the unseen dead and share the feast with them.

After, when everyone is replete, read poems, play music, sing, or whatever you like to entertain each other. Any children present may want to put on impromptu plays or read their own poems aloud.

Read tarot cards or practice other forms of divination.

With Samhain, the Wheel has come almost full circle. To some people this is the New Year, to others the rebirth of the sun at Yule starts the cycle again.

The seasonal rituals I have given in this chapter are partly built around the concept of incorporating a cycle of personal work and harvest into the festival framework. I have done this to show that the ritual year can be used for personal growth. I would like to make it clear that the Wheel of the Year can be followed as a cycle of celebration and devotion alone, and that it is not obligatory to work magic into the festivals . . . this is a matter of personal choice or need.

The other point is that I have described a Britain that sounds somewhat idyllic. Of course, we don't all have a peaceful rural existence or endless unspoilt landscape; Britain has more than its share of motorways, pollution, and urban overcrowding, with all its attendant problems. But the eight festivals are based on the ancient cycles, and most of us would like to celebrate them in a rural setting if possible; though, of course, many pagans live and practice in towns and cities, and some of us don't even have the benefit of a garden. The spirit of the festivals dwells in the turning seasons that are marked by the greening of nature, the subsequent ebb of the growth energies, and then the rebirth of light and life again. Ours is an earth religion, and even if we celebrate in a busy city, we will do so with the intention of aligning ourselves with the natural cycles that can be felt anywhere: many of us will go into the countryside to perform our rituals or, at least, to bring in the flowers, fruits, and greenery appropriate to the season.

The last point is that nature herself is the best teacher we can have when we first begin to follow the pagan festivals. We can learn much just from observing the sky, the trees, the behaviour of animals. If we are prepared to open ourselves to its fluctuating energies, then we will feel the tide of the year as it rises and falls. At the moment, at least in Britain, the seasons are distorted, bringing mild winters and hot summers, but even so, the patterning of the seasons is still discernable; and I firmly believe that celebrating the ancient celebratory dates, along with educating people about care for the environment, can help to gradually right the balance.

CHAPTER EIGHT

Magical Practice

Magic is the energy through which we alter our circumstances and our inner selves. Magic is growth, for even when you use it for banishing or diminishing something, you are developing in psychological, emotional, and spiritual terms by the act of directing your own process. Magic is brought about by a mixture of thought, visualisation, and belief. Many years ago, when I attended Spiritualist sessions, the mediums had a saying: Thought has matter. By this they meant that thoughts that are given power by strong belief or constant repetition can become reality. People say, "Think positive," because we all have an inbuilt instinctive belief in the power of thought to bless or blight our lives. So magic is an art and a craft, a science and a skill, and yet it is entirely natural, and all of us use it from time to time whether we know it or not. In witchcraft we choose to use it deliberately, to develop our unconscious abilities so that we can have more control over the way our lives unfold.

The energy we use in magic fluctuates with the ebb and flow of the moon's different phases, and so a particular type of magical work needs to be timed for the appropriate point in the moon's cycle, and this was dealt with in chapter 6, "The Moon"; though remember that you need to banish adverse circumstances on the waning moon and work for increase or concrete goals on the waxing to full moon. Other factors come into play as well, and these include: the seasons; whether one of the eight festivals is happening or imminent; astrological factors; the day of the week, and even the hour of the day; one's own level of energy and personal circumstances, health, and so on; solar activity, including eclipses and sun spots. It is also necessary to take into account the appropriate colours, particularly when using cord or candle magic.

Magic works, but it doesn't always work consistently, and sometimes it appears to fail altogether. By taking the above mentioned variables into consideration, we can make the best possible use of our magical efforts, timing them to take advantage of beneficent circumstances and trying to avoid conditions that will block our efforts.

With all spell craft, it is up to you whether or not you work within a cast circle. It is perfectly possible to obtain satisfactory results without setting up a proper circle—indeed, I have heard of people doing spontaneous magic while sitting in a crowded pub or in a traffic jam. However, a properly constructed circle has the advantage of acting like a container, concentrating the power and holding it in until it is ready to be sent. At the very least, it might be wise to cast a circle of protection round yourself mentally, asking each of the quarters to be present, as this will provide some protection from distractions and random negativity.

Every object that you use in a spell (with the exception of earth or seeds and other organic matter that should be blessed instead) should first be consecrated through the elements, otherwise unwanted energies may spoil your work. Take your cords or candle or other "props" and pass them clockwise through the elements in turn, three consecutive times each: first the lighted incense for air, then a candle flame for fire, then sprinkle with water, then with salt for earth. Say, in turn, "I consecrate thee with air (then fire, water, earth)." With organic matter, hold it in your hands and ask the Goddess and God to bless and cleanse it ready for use; say something like, "May the Lady and the Lord bless and cleanse these seeds/this earth (or whatever), that they may be fit for my purpose. Blessed be."

Assume that you will always need to consecrate objects for use in spells, either prior to your rite or during it. With candles you also have the choice of priming them with oil, for which olive oil, sunflower oil, or almond oil are ideal. You don't have to do this, but stroking a candle with oil helps to charge it with energy, especially if you concentrate on your magical intent while you do so. The oil should be used sparingly and stroked on from tip to centre and base to centre, which helps to draw power into the candle (unless you are doing a banishing spell, in which case you should apply from the centre outward). Some oils are specific to particular magical goals, whether as part of candle magic or generally, and include the following:

Camphor for psychic protection (particularly good to use when invaded by negative thoughts from someone else).

Cinnamon for warmth, energy, and money spells.

Clove for warmth, stimulation, or sexuality.

Eucalyptus for protection and purification, and to heal head, throat, or chest complaints.

Frankincense for purification and to increase creativity and spirituality, or prosperity.

Lavender for purification, protection, healing and peace, or to promote sleep.

Myrrh for protection or purification.

Patchouli for prosperity and money spells, and for male fertility.

Rose to bring love or friendship, or to promote a sense of harmony and well-being, and for female sexuality.

Rosemary for healing and to aid memory or pay tribute to the dead.

Sandalwood for protection, or as an aid to meditation and spiritual work.

Vanilla for well-being, and for women wanting to attract sexuality.

There are many more, and you need to read widely, especially the tables of correspondences in occult books, and use your intuition to compile your own list of magical oils.

Whether you use candles, cords, seeds, or other objects in your spells, these things are just symbols that help your mind to focus on the desired outcome. The most important factor in working successful magic is intent, and it is possible to bring about results by thought alone and by believing that what you want will happen. However, most of us find that having something to concentrate on and pour our energies into helps us to believe in the effectiveness of what we are doing, and so we tie knots in a cord, or prime and charge a candle. Along with these actions, we use strong visualisation. Before you can work toward a goal, you have to have a clear idea of what it is you want to bring about. You also need to "see" what your life will be like when the outcome is

attained. Visualising your goal is just as important as believing in it. If you have strong doubts and misgivings about
what you are doing, or if you are half-hearted about it, then
it is probable that your magic will fail or will be inconclusive
or incomplete in some way.

Another vitally important factor revolves around ethics.
In magic, it is entirely wrong to work against the will of
another, even if you think it would be in their best interests
(and this includes spells to make someone love or like you,
or have sex with you), or to ask for anything that might
harm someone else or, indeed, yourself. Wording is very
important here, though ultimately it is intent that counts
the most, but while I don't believe that a carelessly worded
spell will bring dire results if your intention was pure, it
doesn't do any harm to play safe. Certainly, it isn't a good
idea to ask for money (or anything else) at any cost . . . and
I was horrified when I once heard somebody do this.
Receiving compensation because of a bad car accident or
industrial accident is not the best way to solve your finan-
cial problems.

The other issue revolves around healing. We don't have
the right to heal someone without their permission or
knowledge, no matter how appropriate it may seem to do so.
How can you really know what another person needs? The
exception might be a child or someone ill enough to have
lost consciousness for a period of time; but even in these circumstances it would be best to work by sending them love
and asking that they receive your healing if that's what is
right for them. Similarly, don't wish better circumstances for
somebody else unless they ask you to . . . in other words,
don't take it upon yourself to meddle in another's life.

The last point is that magic is not a substitute for practical
action. If you can solve a problem by your own efforts, then
do so. Magic works via an energy exchange anyway, and
there is little point in putting a lot of time and effort into

finding a new job by magical means when you haven't even bothered to look in the local paper.

Personal Circumstances

It's very unwise to attempt to work magic when you are ill or emotionally unbalanced, as you will drain yourself and produce possibly unwholesome results. If you are tired or unwell, you can gain a lot of benefit from being present in the circle if others are prepared to build sacred space and perform ritual around you with the aim of healing you, but it would not be a good time for them to also perform other forms of magic, as your negative state could be counterproductive. Similarly, if you practice as a solitary, don't try to cast a circle, but merely light candles and incense and sit quietly for a while, drawing energy into yourself from the air around you and the earth beneath you; then ask the powers of good in the universe to heal you . . . or just go outside and benefit from sunlight or moonlight, and leave magical work until you are better.

It is my personal opinion that it's a bad idea to work when you are extremely drunk or stoned; you very likely won't be able to do so in a controlled and ethical manner. Some people may argue with this viewpoint, but I can only speak from my own perspective and from my experience of encountering the negative effects of careless work done by people who were under the influence of drugs and alcohol. This is not to say that the controlled use of drugs and herbs by genuinely shamanic peoples is invalid, but remember that ritual intoxication is a part of their spiritual culture, and they have centuries of experience behind them and always use mind-altering substances in controlled conditions.

Coming into circle to practice magic when you are emotionally upset is a bad idea as well. If you are in need emotionally, then light a candle and sit before your shrine or in another quiet space and ask for healing, peace, and a resolution to your problems, or go out for a walk or sit in the garden; but don't try to work magically until you have calmed down. The same goes for states of extreme emotional hyperactivity. I can't stress enough that to work responsible magic, you need to be calm and centred, and this is one purpose of the grounding and centring we do before the circle is cast; then any energy raised is used in a careful and purposeful way. If your energies are all over the place, you won't be able to direct them sensibly or you may be less than careful with your wording and visualisation, and may consequently end up with unexpected and unwelcome results. This is not to say that reaching the end of your tether over something can't produce the burst of energy needed to unblock you and help you move beyond restrictions, but simply that successful magic requires you to be focused, and emotional upset often has the effect of diluting one's sense of purpose and determination.

Leave at least an hour and a half between eating and performing any kind of magical ritual. The reason for this is that food is grounding and firmly closes your chakras, so it is difficult to raise energy or enter a state of mind conducive to magical work when you are dulled and heavy with food.

Astrological and Planetary Influences

If you want to be very precise about your work, then study astrology and get ahold of a table of planetary hours, because aligning your work with the activities of the heavens can fine-tune it. For instance, if you have Jupiter making a beneficent contact with an area of your birth chart, then it may be a good time to work a spell of increase, especially concerning money or lucky breaks, though you would need to keep an eye on the details. If you were also to work on the day of the week and during the time of day ruled by Jupiter, then you would be increasing the efficiency of the spell, though it would have to be performed on a waxing or full moon as well. Jupiter, of course, can also be helpful with spiritual work or travel.

Conversely, Saturn and its day and hour would be best used for working on conditions that need to be contained or restricted in some way, or for building a solid, firm structure for something.

The sun is concerned with health, wealth, growth, and creativity; the moon with home and domestic issues and psychic activity; Mercury with communication, short-distance travel, and buying and selling; Mars with combativeness, stimulation, and success; Venus with love, friendship, and enjoyment; Uranus with intuitiveness and sudden creative insights, as well as modern technologies; Neptune with poetry, dance, and meditation, and with spiritual work of a deeply psychic nature; Pluto with death (symbolically) and rebirth, psychological states, and matter surfacing from the subconscious depths.

You can also find out which astrological sign the moon occupies at a particular time, and the current sun sign, both of which will have some bearing on your working.

If you want to make use of astrological factors, then you need to read a lot about astrology and learn to cast and interpret your own birth chart. Then make a note of your own current transits when planning magical work. This is a vast and ever-unfolding subject that takes time to understand in any useful depth, but it is worth the effort and hard work needed to learn it.

The Days of the Week

The names of our days are a mixture of Roman and Norse deities and their Anglo-Saxon equivalents, with the exception of Sunday and Monday, which are named for the sun

and moon, respectively. Each day has (via planetary associa-
tion) its own set of correspondences, including metals, gemstones, oils, and incenses, and these can be employed in
magical rituals if you wish.

Sunday

This is the sun's own day. Sunday is the day on which to
work for health or money, for enjoyment of a creative or dramatic nature, or for prosperity and success in general.

Colour: gold, orange, yellow

Metal: gold

Gem: yellow topaz, golden citrine

Incense: frankincense, copal, rosemary

Oil: bergamot, orange, frankincense, olive, rosemary

Flower or herb: marigold, sunflower, angelica, bay, mistletoe,
rosemary

Tree: olive, oak

Monday

Monday is ruled by the moon. It is devoted to motherhood,
family, the past, tradition, clairvoyance, and other forms of
psychic activity.

Colour: silver, violet, white

Metal: silver

Gem: moonstone

Incense: damiana, lotus, coconut, artemisia, jasmine

Oil: lotus, lemongrass, jasmine, lemon

Flower or herb: artemisia, lotus, jasmine

Tree: willow

Tuesday

Tuesday is named for the Norse god Tyr, Anglicised as Tew, whose Roman counterpart was Mars. It is a day for fresh beginnings and determined activity, for fighting for ones rights, for growth and success, especially when winning out against opposition, and for male sexuality.

Colour: red

Metal: iron

Gem: ruby, diamond, bloodstone

Incense: allspice, tobacco, dragonsblood, cinnamon

Oil: pepper, cinnamon

Flower or herb: basil, poppy, coriander, ginger, thistle

Tree: holly

Wednesday

Wednesday is named for the Norse god Odin and his Saxon counterpart Wodin, but it is also ruled by Mercury. It is a day for commercial transactions, for buying and selling, for successful communication, and for mental activity, including new ideas and fast thinking.

Colour: yellow

Metal: mercury (don't use this in spells, as it is extremely toxic)

Gem: yellow citrine, agate, sardonyx

Incense: lavender

Oil: lavender, almond

Flower or herb: lavender, marjoram

Tree: hazel, almond

Thursday

This day belongs to Thor, but it is also presided over by Jupiter. It is a day to work on travel, writing or spiritual growth, wisdom and learning.

Colour: purple, royal blue

Metal: tin

Gem: turquoise, topaz, lapis lazuli

Incense: cedar, clove, sage

Oil: cedar, clove, nutmeg (don't take nutmeg oil internally, as it is toxic except in very small quantities)

Flower or herb: clove, sage, borage

Tree: cedar, chestnut, oak

Friday

This is Freya's day. She is the Norse goddess of love and fertility, whose Roman counterpart is Venus. This day can be used magically for spells involving love and friendship, harmony, pleasure, and enjoyment. It is involved with female sexuality.

Colour: all shades of pink and rose, mauve, spring green, soft blue

Metal: copper

Gem: emerald, sapphire, rose quartz, malachite

Incense: benzoin, rose

Oil: benzoin, rose, apricot, lilac, vanilla

Flower or herb: daisy, rose, lilac

Tree: apple, in particular, and most fruit trees in general

Saturday

This day belongs to the Roman god Saturn, and it is concerned with restriction, convention, building the framework for something, and banishing unwanted conditions.

Colour: gray, brown, dark green, black

Metal: lead

Gem: jet, obsidian, basalt

Incense: sulphur, myrrh, patchouli

Oil: myrrh, cypress, patchouli

Flower or herb: comfrey, ivy, elder

Tree: cypress, elder

Not only are the days of the week ruled by the planets, but the hours of the day are as well. Serious magicians will time their workings to take both into account, along with any current astrological factors. However, it is perfectly possible to largely ignore astrological factors and the days of the week and still attain successful results with your spells, though a working knowledge of the current pattern of the heavens can help you to avoid particularly difficult or obstructive times.

Bear in mind, also, that there are many different tables of correspondences, both in serious occult tomes and popular books on magic and witchcraft; not all of these sources will agree, and some of them may use more than one connection between correspondences, so that, for example, the oak tree may be attributed to both the sun and Jupiter. As always, it's best to use your intuition when compiling your own set of correspondences . . . and sometimes only trying things out will clarify what works best for you.

The eight festivals mark significant points on the cycle of the year, and this was dealt with fully in chapter 7. Timing your work to coincide with the unfolding seasons and the festivals can help when planning magic, though obviously this is not always practical or even possible. If you need to increase something now, and it's the middle of winter, there is little point in waiting until the spring and summer months. However, if you want to work on long-range goals, then aligning them with the rise and fall of the seasonal cycle makes sense.

A seeding time is from Yule, or Winter Solstice, to Oestara, or Spring Equinox. The forces of growth that have been dormant during the winter months are coming alive again now. You can begin to formulate ideas from Yule onward, then cleanse your life of the old at Imbolc so that your new "seeds" can be planted at Oestara. The work can be carefully tended and nurtured during the summer months, and harvested at Lammas, when any failed projects can be discarded. From the Autumn Equinox until the following Yule, you can assess what you have gained, release what you don't need, then turn your attention inward to your emotional and spiritual needs. In a sense, you will be applying the same principles to your magical work as our ancestors applied to the agricultural round.

As spells and rituals for the festivals were expanded upon in the relevant chapter, I will give only a brief breakdown here in the way of a reminder.

Yule

Yule is the turning point of the year, when the creative upsurge begins again and the light is reborn. Magically, this is the best time to assess ourselves and our lives with a view to formulating new patterns and goals for the year ahead.

Ideas may just be beginning to stir in our unconscious minds, or we may have some fresh endeavours that we want to try out, but this is not the time to push them into full realisation; rather, it is the space in which we let the energies slowly expand and build.

Imbolc

Now we can make a clean sweep, symbolically purifying our lives of anything we have grown beyond, all the clutter and residue that the inward self-examination of winter has thrown up. We can express our new wishes now, in this time of conception, of germination, and concentrate our attention and energy into fresh projects.

Oestara

This is the time to plant our ideas, which is why seed magic is so popular at this time of spring newness. We are no longer looking for goals, but are ready to tend our fully-formed intentions.

Beltane

Everything is flowering and productive, though the time of harvest is still far off. Beltane produces a great burst of energy that helps things along. We can reinforce the purification of Imbolc by jumping over the Beltane Bonfire, then reaffirm our goals by concentrating extra power into them.

Summer Solstice

Things are almost ripe now, but not quite. It is a time to redouble our efforts of nurturing goals along, whilst enjoying the peak of mellow energy that this season brings.

Lammas

Now is the harvest. We can give thanks for those things that have succeeded, and examine those that have failed or have

not yet borne fruit. Some things have to be released from
our lives, while others need a little more love and care to
come to fruition.

Autumn Equinox

This is the second harvest. Those goals that had not ripened
at Lammas may be ready now; others will have to be relin-
quished, and still others carried over and examined to see
how they can be worked on later. As the energy returns to
the soil, so we begin the inward journey of self-examination
that will help us to work more effectively when the light
half of the year returns.

Samhain

Although the forces of light have not yet waned fully, this is
the point of death, the end of summer, the best time of all to
descend to the underworld of our inner selves so that we might
make the realisations that will help us when the year turns
again at Yule. This is a chance to honour our dead, both actual
and metaphorical, and let go finally of anything we need to discard. From now on, hope will begin to increase, even though
the light is still diminishing, for we are on the home stretch to
the Winter Solstice and the rebirth of the sun.

Working magically with the festivals, twining our rituals
of celebration in and out of our lunar and magical work, can
make for a satisfying and ultimately stabilising life.

Colour Correspondences for Magical Work

Colour correspondences are a large part of ritual and magical
work. They are allocated to the planets and days of the week,
as has been shown in the earlier part of this chapter, and are
a fundamental ingredient in tarot, astrology, and work with
the elements. Whether you are using candles or cords, or
even crystals and gemstones, selecting the correct colours can

considerably enhance your efforts. Although it is perfectly possible to use white or black candles and cords only, using a wider range of colours will enrich spells and rituals and trigger a deep and instinctive subconscious response, which will enhance your understanding and open psychic doors.

The following is a basic set of colour correspondences, but it pays to research this subject as widely as possible and add to or alter the list to suit yourself.

Red

Passion, courage, strength, purpose, vitality, health, male sexuality, basic survival, anger, lust, warmth, rapid healing. Use red cautiously, as it is not a gentle colour to work with, and results may happen dramatically and with a lack of regard for finer feelings.

Orange

Ambition, confidence, success in career or material concerns, money, cheerfulness, creativity, well-being, strength, but of a gentler kind than red.

Yellow

Intellectual or mental work, communications, study, exams.

Green

Prosperity, healing, fertility, nature, trees, growth (spring or paler greens work quickly, darker shades are more consolidating).

Blue

Light blue for peace and tranquillity, dark blue for meditation and spiritual understanding, all shades for harmony and understanding, detachment, and healing mental stress.

Purple

Travel, writing, learning, higher education, wisdom, spiritual growth and understanding, power, ambition; violet shades are useful to promote the frame of mind for meditation or clairvoyance.

Mauve/Lilac/Lavender

Well-being and enjoyment of a calm and harmonious kind, comfort.

Pink

Female sexuality, dark pink for passion, light pink for love and friendship, harmony, enjoyment, well-being.

Brown

Earth energy, the winter soil, stability, grounding material goals into reality.

Gold

Money, prosperity, wealth, enjoyment, luxury, the sun.

Silver

Purity, tranquillity, detachment, purification, protection, the moon, psychic and clairvoyant activity.

White

A universal colour that can be used for any work, but particularly for purification, protection, peace, spirituality, the moon.

Black

Banishing (particularly negative conditions), releasing, weight loss, to absorb negativity, grounding and centring, the waning and dark moon.

In addition to the colour correspondences, you may find it useful to research and apply the colours and meanings of crystals and gemstones to your magic. A brief list is given below, but this is a field of study that has a whole category to itself in occult and new age bookshops; so, if you find yourself attracted to this area, it's worth reading as much as you can and building up your own personal set of meanings.

Amber

Amber is an orange/yellow resin that is fossilised pine sap. It is a cleansing and balancing stone, which helps to get vital energies flowing properly around the system and purifies the aura. It is warming and gentle in its effect. Be aware that a lot of amber currently being sold contains a large proportion of plastic resin, so old amber is probably a better bet.

Astrological rulership: yellow shades belong to Leo, and orange shades belong to Taurus.

Chakra: yellow shades belong to the solar plexus, and orange shades to the navel chakra.

Amethyst

A member of the quartz family, amethyst varies in colour from pale violet to deep purple. It is used for spiritual and psychic development, and to help in meditation or to induce sleep. It is also a healing stone.

Astrological rulership: Pisces.

Chakra: the deeper shades belong to the third eye, and the paler shades to the crown chakra.

Aquamarine

A clear gemstone that is pale green-blue or sea blue in colour. It is used for psychic development, for the ability to speak out, and for healing throat problems. It helps to purify the aura and cleanse the throat chakra of blockages, and has an overall balancing effect. Wearing it can help you to attune to the sea and the concept of the Goddess as the maternal ocean of being.

Astrological rulership: Gemini and Pisces.

Chakra: the throat and third eye (or brow) chakra.

Carnelian

This is a reddish-orange, translucent, semiprecious stone with a touch of pink. It is grounding, earthing, and healing (especially to the digestive system), and helps us to connect to the here and now and the worldly circumstances in which we find ourselves, giving us the strength and energy to cope with our everyday lives. It is a stone that was used frequently by the ancient Egyptians.

Astrological rulership: Taurus.

Chakra: navel.

Citrine

This stone is a member of the quartz family. The darker shades are a brownish-orange, the lighter shades range from pale, almost straw-coloured yellow to rich amber-gold. Much citrine on the market is really amethyst that has been baked to change it from purple to bronze, though these crystals are still quite effective in use. Deep-orange citrine helps to regulate the digestive system; it also connects us to the navel chakra and grounds us into the material world. Citrine can be used in spells to attract material prosperity. The lighter yellow shades help to calm the solar plexus, soothing nervousness and anxiety, and so it is a good stone to carry before an interview or exam.

Astrological rulership: the lighter shades belong to Gemini, the mid-shades to Leo, and the deeper shades to Taurus.

Chakra: yellow crystals belong to the solar plexus, and the deeper colours to the navel chakra.

Jasper

This is an opaque, earth-red stone that is useful for grounding and for restoring basic, vital energy. It can be used to help cleanse the liver. It has protective qualities when worn, shielding the aura from negativity.

Astrological rulership: Taurus.

Chakra: the base chakra.

Lapis Lazuli

This varies in shade from a deep, dark blue, through rich, royal blue, to a mid-blue with hints of turquoise and violet. The stone is opaque and often has flecks of gold-coloured iron pyrites embedded in it, and may contain streaks of white. In medieval times, it was the precious ingredient used to make blue pigment . . . very sparingly used because it was so costly. Lapis is a deeply spiritual stone, helping to cleanse and develop both the throat chakra and the third eye. It instills wisdom and harmony, and is therefore very useful to wear during meditation.

Astrological rulership: Sagittarius.

Chakra: throat and third eye.

Malachite

This is an opaque green stone containing banded streaks and swirls of paler green, often in marbled or bull's-eye patterns, or spirals. Its surface is often coated with minute clear quartz crystals. This mineral connects us with the earth and nature. It is healing for the heart, and also the eyes and throat, and can be worn to protect one from negative energies. Malachite was sacred in ancient Egyptian times, when it was carved into talismans and jewelry, and ground down to mix into eye shadow (a dangerous practice, as it contains toxins).

Astrological rulership: Taurus and Capricorn.

Chakra: the heart and throat chakras.

Obsidian

This mineral is a deep purplish-black, semi-opaque volcanic glass; some obsidian has white flecks, earning it the name of snowflake obsidian. It links the base chakra with the crown chakra. Obsidian is a very powerful stone that helps us to bring past pain and suffering to the surface of our minds, where we can face it and then transmute it, thereby growing spiritually. It also helps us to develop inner vision, insight, and understanding.

Astrological rulership: Scorpio and Capricorn.

Chakra: the base chakra, the third eye, and the crown chakra.

Quartz

These days, most people are familiar with clear quartz crystals, as they are the most popular and most widely written about minerals of the new age culture, and fantastic claims have been made for them . . . ranging from their having been transported here from other galaxies, to being repositories of encoded wisdom willed into them telepathically by the priests of doomed Atlantis. I leave it to you to judge the genuine nature of such claims.

Quartz is an energiser and a cleanser. Wearing clear quartz can charge you with earth energy and etheric power. The aura can be cleansed by passing the tip of a quartz point over the entire etheric field from head to toe, or by concentrating on the chakra points—though if you decide to cleanse yourself or someone else in this way, then be sure to close the chakras afterward by eating something or by visualising each centre closing one at a time in sequence. Quartz also transmits energies, so a person holding a crystal can, often inadvertently, project their thoughts, emotions, and auric signature to the people in close proximity to them.

Quartz can also be placed with a spell to energise and protect it while it is underway. Put a clear quartz crystal at the base of a spell candle or on top of a piece of writing, for example. Clear quartz is also a great aid in psychic and spiritual development. It opens the clairvoyant centres and balances the whole aura. A magical circle cast with a quartz crystal will be especially powerful, precise, and strong.

Astrological rulership: Capricorn and Pisces.

Chakra: the crown chakra.

Rose Quartz

This beautiful, semi-opaque, noncrystalline form of quartz is a healer for the heart and emotions. It is gentle, soft, and protective, and is the ideal stone to be carried by people who are lonely or have suffered a great deal of emotional pain or bereavement.

Astrological rulership: Taurus.

Chakra: the heart.

Turquoise

This is a greenish-blue opaque stone that has been used through the ages by many cultures, including the ancient Egyptians, Tibetans, Mexican native peoples, Arabs, and Native Americans. It is often used in jewelry, or else carried as a stone of protection against negativity and bad luck. It helps with throat and eyesight problems. The Arabs believe that it will guard one against accidents whilst travelling, and, because of this, turquoise was often sewn on to the bridles of horses. In modern times, it can be seen dangling from the dashboards of vehicles in Middle Eastern countries. Turquoise can help you to connect to the spiritual realms whilst remaining grounded and balanced.

Astrological rulership: Taurus and Sagittarius.

Chakra: the throat and third eye.

This is a small sampling of the many crystals and gemstones that can be used in magical and healing work. It is worth bearing in mind, when acquiring minerals to work with, that our recent interest in these things for healing and psychic work has caused their value to skyrocket. Many poor countries are now being strip-mined to provide the rich West with crystals, and this not only disfigures the landscape and violates the earth our Mother, but often deprives indigenous peoples of their land and homes. If you want to buy minerals, try to find out their source. There are still ethical companies providing materials for the market. Often stones from mass mining are traumatised and disfigured because of the explosives used to obtain them, and these specimens are difficult to work with anyway.

Putting It All Together

The best way to explain magic in use is to describe various spells and how to work them. The following are several different spells, which, between them, use a cross-section of some of the techniques described in the main body of the chapter.

A Simple Prosperity Spell

You can cast a circle and raise energy, or simply do this spell at your altar or shrine without making any particular preparations.

You will need:

- A fresh green candle
- A candle holder
- Altar candles
- Matches or lighter
- Patchouli oil
- A censer or other fireproof container with charcoal
- Frankincense incense or a mixture containing patchouli
- A bowl of water
- A container of salt

Light the altar candles and charcoal block for incense.

While the charcoal is igniting, sit quietly and breathe deeply and calmly to ground and centre yourself.

Place some incense on the charcoal.

Consecrate the green candle through the elements, then prime it with patchouli oil (as explained before), concentrating hard on your magical goal as you do so, voicing it in your mind over and over again, putting emphasis and energy into the words.

Now hold the candle to your third eye and concentrate hard on visualising prosperity; see how circumstances will be for you when the needed prosperity arrives; be very determined; *believe* that your desire will come about; specify that it happens in a way that is right for you and harms no one, including yourself. Will energy into the candle so that your visualisation is empowered.

When you feel you have done enough visualisation, light the green candle from the altar candles, saying:

**I light this candle to bring prosperity into my life.
To the free will of all and the highest
good of all concerned.**

Let the candle burn for a while (if you are doing this spell as part of another rite, then until the end of the ritual will do). When you snuff it out, visualise prosperity as though it is already a part of your life.

Relight the candle every night for a predetermined period of time. A good length is until the end of the moon's cycle; in other words, until just before the next new moon. If you feel you need more time to reinforce the spell, then rekindle the candle nightly until the moon returns to the same phase in which you started—for example, if you began the spell two days before the full moon, then let it run until two days before the next full moon. Try to work out how much to burn each night, but make sure the candle is completely consumed by the end of the final lighting. As you relight it, restate your magical intention, though you needn't repeat the whole affirmation; just the word "prosperity" will do. Then, each time you extinguish it, briefly refresh your visualisation of improved circumstances.

This spell could equally be done using an orange candle and cinnamon oil. Use your intuition about which combination to go for. I've used both, myself, in the past. Using orange helps you to be more determined if you are feeling unsure about whether the spell will succeed, and green is a good choice if you're prepared to let things flow in a gentle manner, coming to fruition in good time.

Prosperity spells tend to work quite well most of the time. If you are blocking to any extent, then your rewards may come in small ways. Someone I know, who didn't really believe the prosperity spell he had done could change his circumstances, sold some secondhand goods and found a bunch of gift-wrapped flowers and a small amount of money in the street, all on the same day. This gave him enough faith in the power of magic to allow the block to dissolve, so that reinforcing the working at a later date gave him the chance of a new job with a considerable raise in pay.

Spell to Bring a Needed Sum of Money

If you need a specific sum of money urgently, then this is a useful spell. If you want, you can place yellow and orange flowers on your altar during the working, and burn gold candles.

You will need to do this spell on a Sunday, during a waxing or full moon, but in daylight. If you want to fine-tune the spell by doing it when the moon is in Leo and during the sun's planetary hour, then this will help as well.

You will need:

- A circle of gold, yellow, or orange cloth about four to six inches in diameter
- A length of gold thread, enough to twist three times round the neck of the cloth when it's gathered to form a bag
- Some coins painted with gold paint or nail varnish, or else small disks of gold card cut out to look like coins (or even some chocolate money, such as is available at Christmas time . . . be inventive!)
- Frankincense with charcoal and burner
- A small piece of citrine (small crystals or polished stones can be bought quite cheaply)
- A pinch of cinnamon

Light any candles and get the incense going, then consecrate all the noncombustible ingredients for the spell through the elements, and bless the others.

Place the gold cloth on your altar, preferably on a pentacle.

Put the "coins" on the cloth, then follow with the citrine and the cinnamon.

Pick up the cloth and its contents and draw the edges up to form a bag or pouch, then hold this in your hands carefully, concentrating on the image of the sum of money you need as you do so, putting all your attention and effort into "seeing" yourself receiving that money and paying for whatever it is you need it for.

Say:

> **The money I need for (purpose) will come to me,**
> **in the names of the Goddess and God**
> **and with harm to none . . .**

Twist the gold thread round the neck of the pouch three times, knotting it each time, and with each knot, say "So mote it be," willing power and determination into the knots as you do so.

Hold the pouch in your hands and say "Blessed be," and then put the spell away in a safe place, preferably in a box or other container on your shrine.

When the spell manifests, untie the pouch and disperse the ingredients. You might want to put them aside for future work.

Spell to Bring Harmony into Your Relationships

This is a useful spell if you are going through a period of conflict with one or more people close to you. Please note that this spell is intended to work on your own equilibrium, not to try to manipulate friends and lovers.

Do this spell on a Friday, during a waxing moon.

You will need:

- A sheet of pink paper
- A pink or mauve pen or crayon
- A small piece of rose quartz

- A pink rose for the altar (optional)
- A pink candle in a fairly pale shade
- Candle holder
- Benzoin incense with burner and charcoal
- Water and salt for consecration

Light the pink candle and get the incense going.

Consecrate and bless the spell materials as usual, then sit still and quiet for several minutes, breathing the scent of the incense and becoming calm and relaxed.

Now, using the pink or mauve pen or crayon, write the word "Harmony" on the paper and fold it over several times to form a small, flat packet.

Hold this in your hands and concentrate on the feeling of harmony, balance, and peace. Remember, you aren't trying to gloss over feelings of anger and resentment between you and another, but are just working on your own inner need for emotional tranquillity and balance, and love.

Now say the following invocation:

**Lady Venus, I ask that you bring your blessings to
my rite and love and harmony to my life;
that my relationships can blossom free of conflict.**

Place the pink candle in its holder on top of the folded paper, and put the rose quartz at the base of the candle.

Put these things somewhere safe and leave the candle to burn out.

When the candle has burned down, put the paper in a box on your shrine and leave it.

Scrape any wax off the rose quartz and carry the stone on your person (you can buy or make a small pouch to hang it round your neck if you like, or put it in a pocket). Keep it with you day and night for a while.

This spell can be adapted to bring love or friendship . . . but not, I stress, the love or friendship of a specific individual!

Spell to Work on Career

This spell can be used to bring a new career direction or to improve an existing career path.

You will need:

- The usual equipment for consecrating a spell (altar candles and so on)
- A length of orange cord (you can use the type that is sold in haberdashery departments and intended for upholstery binding. It should be in a measurement of three, or a multiple of three of a measurement that is long enough to work with comfortably [three feet is usual, or nine feet—which is a three times three]; the reason for the three-times measurement is because three is a number sacred to the Goddess)

Consecrate your cord through the elements.

Sit and focus on your magical goal, visualising it strongly, holding the cord in your hand and willing energy into it, pouring your thoughts along the path of power the energy forms. Feel the power really flowing out through your hands and into the cord until you feel you have done all you can.

Now tie a knot in the exact middle of the cord, pulling it tight, concentrating on your goal as you do so. Then say:

I've knotted one, the spell's begun.

The next knot is tied at the extreme end of the left hand side of the cord, and the words are:

I've knotted two, it cometh true.

The rest of the knot tying sequence is as follows.

Extreme right:

I've knotted three, so will it be.

Midway between left and centre:

I've knotted four, its strength is more.

Midway between right and centre:

I've knotted five, it comes alive.

Midway between the leftmost knots:

I've knotted six, the spell to fix.

Midway between the rightmost knots:

I've knotted seven, the stars of heaven.

Midway between the centre knot and the one next left:

I've knotted eight, and seal its fate.

Midway between the centre knot and the one next right:

I've knotted nine, and make it mine.

(As you say this last, try to be determined, to really believe in the truth of the words.)

Now put the cord away somewhere safe. You can leave it and forget about it, or you can untie the knots and cleanse the cord once the goal has manifested.

This is but a small sample of the type of spells you can use. Be as creative as you like, as long as you remain careful and ethical. And remember that some magic needs to be reinforced to help it along, especially if you are dealing with a complex situation, or circumstances that have built up over a period of time. So be prepared to repeat spells that appear to have failed—though give a few weeks for them to work—or try a different type of spell. I find that cord spells often take longer to do their work, but are more solid, whereas candle magic can work quite quickly. How you work really depends on the requirements of a particular situation; and only experimentation, practice, and experience (with a good helping of intuition) will help you find the right combinations.

CHAPTER NINE

Divination

Divination and healing are part of the work many witches do, either in the circle or as separate activities. Some witches earn a living by taking on clients for healing or counselling. Both of these activities are part of magical practice in the sense that they utilise etheric energy and the chakras.

There is a lot of altruistic idealism attached to the subject of doing this type of work for money. I spent years giving astrological readings to people free of charge because I felt it was wrong to use spiritual gifts for material gain (and at that time I didn't have a computer programme to calculate charts, so I was adding an hour or more of calculation time to the two or three hours spent discussing the chart). This is rubbish! If you are working hard and giving up your time, not to mention having strangers invade your living space, then you are entitled to charge a reasonable fee for your efforts; or do some sort of skill swap or other exchange. Money is just another form of energy, and the effort you put into doing a reading or a healing session is being exchanged for the effort your client put into earning the money. I personally found people didn't value my work until I put a price on it, or that receiving something for nothing made them feel obligated and uncomfortable. By all means, have a sliding scale of fees so that those who are financially strapped can still benefit from your help. I would never turn anyone away because they couldn't afford help, but equally, I will no longer put myself in the position of being exploited. After all, you wouldn't expect your dentist or doctor or other professional to treat you without charging you.

Just a cautious word: don't see unknown clients alone. Have someone else in the house while you do the work. Most people are trustworthy, but it would be very unwise to invite a stranger into your home unless there is someone else there to help you if trouble arises. And don't try to help someone who is clearly severely mentally disturbed, unless you have training and experience in psychological counselling.

The other factor to take into consideration is that of free will. If you send healing to someone, or if you do a tarot reading (or some other form of clairvoyance or divination) either without their knowledge or without their permission, then you are trespassing. It doesn't matter how justified you think you are, don't do it!

Divination

Divination is the art and skill of examining probable future trends by means outside of those our culture considers normal and rational. It includes the use of scrying tools, tarot cards, runes, the Chinese I Ching or Book of Changes, and several other less-popular methods of reading that include

throwing shells, bones, or pebbles, and deciphering the way
they fall. It is also possible to read shapes in the clouds, in
patterns in the flames of a fire, or in smoke or in the flight of
birds—we have all heard the magpie chant that begins "One
for sorrow, two for joy." In ancient times, people read the
entrails of animals or birds, or ritually slaughtered a human
victim and read the pattern of his or her death throes.

People have very strange ideas about what divination can
and can't do. At one extreme are those who think it doesn't
work because it has no perceivable scientific basis. At the
other extreme are those gullible souls who think that everything is fated and fixed, and that divination shows us a course
that we cannot change. Divination allows us to examine a
map of our inner workings at a given moment in time. It
shows us the factors that have a bearing on our current life
situations, and the way those factors will shape our direction
if we do nothing to change them. The value of any form of
divination is in the insights it can give us. We should not be
asking what will happen, but rather what will happen if . . .

You can do readings for yourself, and this is a good way to
aid self-examination and self-realisation. You can also benefit sometimes from having someone else look at a particular
problem on your behalf.

Divination can be used for almost any question. I have
even used tarot to look into previous lives, though it worked
by showing the character traits and the choices that I had
carried over to this life. Don't, however, expect to be given a
cut-and-dried solution to problems; divination gives you certain insights, certain tools that can be used to work on life
situations or make relevant choices, but it can't wave a magic
wand and make all your troubles go away without any effort
on your part.

If you use tarot cards, or runes, or use coins or yarrow
sticks with the I Ching, it's best to keep them somewhere
safe, perhaps in a special box, and in the case of cards,

wrapped in silk, which psychically insulates and protects them. If you leave them out or let others handle them regularly, then they will pick up all sorts of vibrations that will confuse your readings and make them less accurate. When you first acquire new divination tools, it's a good idea to consecrate them through the elements, the way you do with candles and the like, so that they are thoroughly cleansed of the energies they absorbed during manufacture and sale. You might want to dedicate them, too, perhaps "telling" them that they are to aid you from now on.

Try to have some peaceful time before a reading. Obviously, this will already have happened if you are within circle; otherwise, sit quietly in the space where the reading will take place and breathe calmly, grounding and centring yourself. This is especially important if you are very receptive and are doing the reading for someone who is nervous or emotionally upset. It's also best not to eat for a while beforehand, as eating will close your chakras and ground you too much.

With all forms of clairvoyance and divination, you will probably find that working in a group will accelerate your development, because being with others who are also in a psychically receptive frame of mind is very conducive to being aware yourself. This is very much the case when in the circle, after ritual.

Tarot

A tarot deck consists of seventy-eight cards that contain archetypal images that trigger a deep subconscious response. Twenty-two of these images, the Major Arcana, are concerned with profoundly spiritual or psychological issues, while the rest of the deck, the Minor Arcana, deals with everyday life. There are various theories as to the origins of tarot, including: they were wall paintings in the caves used for Egyptian initiations; they were brought from India by Romanies; they were invented in medieval Europe; they were part of a book of ancient wisdom from a lost race. But the truth is that nobody really knows where the tarot originates.

Tarot has to be learned patiently, probably from books. With tarot, you must at least learn the patterns and meanings of some basic layouts. You may find that the cards speak to you and that you are able to read the pictures without learning the meanings; in any case, interpretations alter according to the layout, the proximity of other cards, and the specific position of a particular card. Sometimes a card will reveal a meaning that you had never thought of before—a meaning that is relevant to this reading or person.

If you are of a methodical turn of mind, you may have to go the long way round and learn book interpretations, then do lots and lots of readings over a period of time to build up your own definitions. The spread should be read holistically, anyway, not as a set of separate interpretations. For some people the cards are just a trigger that gets their clairvoyant senses going; to others the pictures on the cards may come alive and appear to move or draw one in; others may get intuitive insights.

Although tradition says cards should be given to you, it's okay to buy your own cards, but choose ones that appeal to you, not just a deck a friend has recommended and that you may not personally like. Don't let other people handle your cards until they are thoroughly impregnated with your own etheric energy, after which you can let others handle them during the course of shuffling if you are reading for them.

Lastly, tarot images can be used in meditation, when you can choose a card to act as a gateway for pathworking, or to gain extra insights into its basic meanings, or to be a focus for qualities you wish to bring into your life.

Runes

Runes are more immediate in their action than tarot cards. Tarot gives layers and layers of meaning, from the surrounding influences, to psychological factors, and even to the way some event in a forgotten past is affecting the subject. Runes, though, seem to cut straight to the point without getting involved in so much peripheral matter. They are Norse and Anglo-Saxon in origin, and consist of twenty-five squares or rounds, or even pebbles or semiprecious stones, twenty-four of which are each inscribed with a different runic symbol and one of which is blank. They can be thrown onto a cloth, drawn at random from a bag, or laid out in configuration similar to tarot spreads.

Scrying

Scrying is much less intuitive than it is clairvoyant. It is the art of divining through gazing into a surface such as crystal, glass, smoke, or flames until the rational mind fades back and the paranormal faculties are allowed to come to the fore. Some people see images in the scrying surface, while others have pictures in their mind, or may simply get feelings or insights. Unlike the tarot, where the images are already there and act to trigger insights, the scenes and pictures seen in scrying are projected onto the screen of the mind.

It is possible to buy crystal balls for scrying, and these are made of either glass or quartz, obsidian, or some other mineral. Some crystal balls are quite large, but I have seen people read from ones that are only an inch or so in diameter. The alternative is to buy or make a witch's mirror. Commercially manufactured ones are made of black glass with an opaque coating on the back. Homemade ones can be crafted quite easily by buying a round clock glass, which will be concave/convex, and coating the convex surface with black household paint. Another method of scrying is

to gaze into a bowl or other deep container of water—some
people like to put a silver coin in the bottom to give the
eyes a point to stare at.

The best way to scry is to sit in a dim room, lit only by
candle flames. Gaze in a relaxed but not fixed way into the
scrying surface, let the eyes defocus slightly, and let the mind
unravel. It may take several sessions to get results, but eventually you will be rewarded. For some, this method of divination may be less accurate than using cards or runes because
some of the images seen may be thrown up by the unconscious, and may have more to do with this than with
prophetic insight.

Healing

The sort of healing done by witches can be effected by lay-
ing hands on the patient and channeling energy into them,
or by working a spell in which they are visualised as happy
and well. Most healing is done by the latter, and may
include banishing a condition such as cancer or inflamma-
tion while the moon is waning, and then working toward a
full return to health as the moon waxes. Although this kind
of healing can bring about miraculous cures, it cannot
replace an amputated or severed body part, nor can it work
at all if the subject is resistant to healing through fear, or the
subconscious wish to remain in a state of ill health.

Above all, psychic or magical healing methods are not
meant to be a substitute for proper medical care—if you
need stitches for an open wound, there is absolutely no
point doing healing instead. Get the injury treated, and
then use alternative methods to speed up the recovery time
and deal with any trauma.

Group healing is often especially successful. The combination of several people together visualising a cure and
then sending energy to that end can be extremely powerful.

Subjects of the healing can be placed in the centre of the circle while the others place their hands on them or direct energy toward them, or they could be somewhere else at the time, and therefore the recipient of absent healing. Whichever it is, they *must* know that they are being healed and must either have asked for help, or have agreed to it. Healing can be included in a group spell session, and the power sent with the cone of raised energy, or it could come about through the use of a candle or cord spell, or other magic. Most methods that are used in other magical workings can be used for healing, too.

Although some people appear to have a natural flair for certain techniques of divination and healing, they can be learned and developed by anybody, though we will each have our own way of working. Like any other skill, you must be patient and prepared to work hard at learning and practicing. Go carefully as well, especially if you are using your newly fledged abilities on behalf of someone else. You must always ask for inner guidance, and you must trust your intuition. Don't be tempted to attempt something beyond your capabilities through fear of appearing inept or letting down another person. Do your best, but don't make claims you can't live up to; and if you aren't sure if something is right, then say so.

Afterword

Being a witch isn't something you do only on full moons and festivals, and maybe when you want to work a spell. It isn't a hobby, either. Nor is it the miraculous answer to all of life's problems, though it will give you the tools to cope better with what life throws at you. In fact, part of the teaching of witchcraft is that life contains both dark and light, sorrow and joy, loneliness and togetherness, friendship and love and solitude. Ultimately, we don't follow ritual, magic, and celebration just for our own benefit and that of our fellow group members or our magical partner; we do it for spiritual growth, for shared joy, and to give something back to the world in which we live.

Following the Wheel of the Year, honouring the phases of the moon, communing with Goddess and God—all these are ways to bring our bodies, our minds, and our souls into harmony with the natural cycles, and by so doing encourage our own development and the balancing of those elements of the year's round that have become unstable. We become more aware of the environment and take better care of it. We also become more fulfilled and satisfied human beings. Our understanding of life and death increases, and we may discover that those things we once thought fearful now seem fascinating or wonderful or profound. Witchcraft is a celebration of life; it gives meaning to existence and a way to cope with pain and loss, as well.

The knowledge that present day witches have to acquire was once a fundamental part of daily life. Our ancestors didn't need to learn about the seasons, about the power of the moon, about the Goddess, God, and magic; these were things sensed and absorbed as part of growing up. I think that the wisdom of our forebears still lives in us all, and that we can uncover it, can integrate it fully into our lives, if we trust in ourselves and are determined . . . and, of course, if it's what we want. The path of the witch is a natural one that has existed for far longer than any other—right back to humankind's earliest days, in fact. For most of us exploring witchcraft, even though our first steps may be faltering, we may have many questions and doubts, and we may want to be reassured that we are doing things the right way, we each have inside us everything we need to build a rich and creative spirituality.

But witchcraft and paganism don't belong only to the past. With the advent of mass communication, which is greater than ever before now that so many people use the Internet and e-mail, the pagan religions are growing extremely fast. Witches need no longer feel isolated or strange. With so many witchcraft related e-mail groups to join and websites to visit, we have become a global community, with witches of all nationalities exchanging views, offering each other support, and forming friendships.

We have come full circle, and the spirituality that served our ancestors is now freely accessible for all who want to embrace it and take it into the future.

Glossary

Alexandrian

Contemporary branch of initiatory Wicca founded by Alex Sanders.

Aradia

Said to be a goddess of Etruscan legend, the daughter of Diana who came to earth to champion the poor and oppressed. She has many of the qualities of Artemis/Diana, but shows a more human face. She is much loved by British Wiccans.

Artemis

The Greek Maiden goddess of the hunt, but also of midwifery. She was a lunar goddess and a goddess of the wild, of nature. Her brother was the sun god Helios/Apollo.

Astral Plane

The plane of existence interpenetrating, but less dense, than the material world. Magical work is thought to take root in the astral prior to becoming manifest in the world of form.

Astrology

The analysis of a person, creature, country, or anything else by plotting the planetary patterns personal to them, and using the resulting "chart" to understand probable traits, character, and so on.

Athame

The ritual knife used to direct energy and cast the circle. It is usually steel, double-bladed, and with a black handle, but can be made of any other metal, stone, and so on, and with any colour for the handle. It is never used to draw blood, and the only thing that should ever be cut with it is the cake at a handfasting.

Aura

The sheath of subtle energy surrounding the body.

Autumn Equinox

One of the eight seasonal festivals. Second harvest. Equal days and nights, but with the nights about to increase in length. Occurs around September 21.

Beltane

One of the eight seasonal festivals. Centres on the marriage of the Flower Maiden and the Horned Lord of the Greenwood. April 30 to May 1.

Besom

Another name for the old-fashioned type of broom, made with twigs attached to a rough branch handle, which witches use to cleanse the perimeter of the sacred circle before ritual.

Bodhran

A round, flat Irish hand drum, played with a double-headed wooden beater. Originally a war drum played to rouse the battle lust of Celtic warriors, the bodhran has a wild, exciting sound that can be used to quickly raise energy for magical work or ritual.

Book of Shadows

A journal of spells, rituals, dreams, meditations, and so on, kept by individual witches. It can be an actual book, a computer file, or an audio tape, for example.

Brighid (also Brigit, Brigid, Bride, Brede)

Irish solar/triple goddess of poetry, healing, and smithcraft, whose special time is the purification festival of Imbolc at the beginning of February. She was christianised as Saint Brigit.

An Eastern spiritual system based on meditation and the aim of either transcending earthly existence (Tibetan and Theravada systems), or becoming spiritually enlightened whilst still in the world (Zen). It is a nontheistic system (in other words, it doesn't subscribe to the belief in deity), but teaches compassion and tolerance.

Candlemass

The name given to the Celtic fire festival of Imbolc when it was absorbed into Christianity. Some modern pagans use the name Candlemass instead of Imbolc. It is the Festival of Lights, when candles are lit to represent the return of the sun's power as a generative force, or, in Christianity, to celebrate the purification of Mary after the birth of Jesus.

Celtic

The Bronze Age pre-Saxon peoples of Europe and the British Isles. They were warriors, seers, and metal workers. The four pagan fire festivals originated with them, as did the Druid priesthood, and they are well-known now for their knotwork decorations. Many inhabitants of Scotland, Ireland, Wales, Cornwall, the Isle of Man, and Brittany (in northern France) are the direct descendants of the Celts, and many other Europeans and people of European ancestry have Celtic blood—which can bestow strongly psychic skills.

Cerridwen

The Crone goddess. She was part of Welsh legend. She owns a cauldron of transformation, and has associations with the underworld.

Chakras

Energy centres in the auric field. Chakra is Hindu for "wheel," and these centres are said to revolve like wheels of force when activated.

Chalice

A goblet or cup used to contain wine, juice, spring water, and so forth at the end of a ritual. It belongs to the element water.

Child of Promise

The reborn Sun God at Yule. Personified by such deities as the Celtic Mabon, the Persian Mithras, and Jesus.

Cone of power

Spiral of active power shaped by witches during magical working. Can also be sphere or pillar shaped.

Corn Bride

A small figure made of wheat or other grain stalks, dressed in white to represent the reviving fertility of the crops at Imbolc.

Corn Mother

Traditionally made from the last sheaf of grain to be harvested. A small figure representing the Goddess as the Mother of the Harvest, who will retreat into the burial mounds until spring comes and the forces of growth stir again.

Coven

A small group of witches who regularly come together to work ritual and/or magic and celebrate the festivals. A close knit coven can become something of a support group for the members, with strong bonds of love, kinship, and family growing between them.

The Craft

Witchcraft, sometimes called the Craft of the Wise.

Crone

The aging, wise woman aspect of the Goddess. Corresponds to the waning moon.

Diana

The Roman counterpart of the Greek goddess Artemis, Lady of the Wild.

Deity

The concept of a divine presence. Can be used to refer to a specific goddess or god form.

Demeter

Greek goddess of the corn and harvest, whose daughter Persephone was abducted by Hades and taken to the underworld. Demeter's grieving for her daughter caused winter to come. It was only by making a pact with Hades to allow Persephone to be restored to the upper world for part of the year that Demeter felt able to let fertility and warmth come back into the world.

Divination

Obtaining insight into a situation or circumstances with the help of one of the intuitive or clairvoyant methods, such as tarot or scrying, in order to read current patterns and probable future trends.

Elements

Part of all magical and spiritual systems. They consist of earth, air, fire, water, and ether, and are a way of experiencing and categorising the way the world we live in interfaces with the sacred.

Ephemeris

Astronomical tables of planetary movements used for the accurate calculation of astrological charts.

Etheric Energy

The psychic energy used to shape the ritual circle.

Evoke

To call forth qualities, such as aspects of deity, from oneself or another person or people during ritual.

Gardnerian

Contemporary branch of initiatory Wicca founded by Gerald Gardner.

GMT

Greenwich Mean Time: the time system based on the Greenwich Observatory, and from which all the world's time zones derive. Astrological calculations have to be converted to GMT or Universal time (which varies from GMT by a few seconds) before a horoscope can be accurately done.

Gnome

Personified symbol for the elemental forces of earth.

Great Mother

The term used to describe the Goddess in ancient times. The Goddess as the land or the world.

Green Man

A foliate face or figure; the male spirit of growth and fertility in nature; a manifestation of the God.

Hag

The Goddess as ancient, wise woman. Symbolised by the dark phase of the moon just before astronomical newness. Can also be a destroyer goddess such as Cerridwen, the Celtic Cailleagh, or Hecate, whose work it is to clear the way for new growth.

Handfasting

A pagan marriage ceremony. In some traditions a handfasting is for a year and a day, after which the couple can either renew their vows or decide to part.

Hecate

The Crone or Hag goddess, though she originated as a Greek lunar goddess; she is the keeper of the family hearth fire. Hecate came to have two roles: by day she was a goddess of farming and fertility, but by night she became the goddess of witches and spirits, the Guardian of the Crossroads—symbolising the helper who aids us to make choices when we come to a turning point in life, or when we need to let something go in order to move on.

Hedgewitch

A witch who usually prefers to work alone or with a partner, often in an earthy way, with an emphasis on herbalism and country lore.

Holly King

Ancient winter aspect of the God.

Horned One

The Horned God of ancient northern Europe. Usually seen with antlers on his head, he was called Herne, Cernunnos, and Cerne. The Horned One can also refer to the Greek god Pan.

Imbolc

The festival of purification. One of the eight seasonal festivals. February 1.

I Ching

The Chinese Book of Changes; an ancient system of guidance and divination that is read via a pattern of lines ascertained by casting coins or sticks. It clearly shows how life situations are transitory, and gives wise judgment on how to solve problems.

Inanna

She was the Sumerian forerunner of the Egyptian Isis. She descended to the underworld, giving up her garments and jewelry a bit at a time, symbolising her relinquishment of all outer protection, body armour, and ego masks, in the search of the self. Like Isis, she is also the Queen of the Heavens and Nature, and is said to wear a rainbow as her necklace, and be crowned with stars, with the crescent moon on her brow. She has her origins in the Great Mother of ancient times, who encompassed earth, heaven, and the underworld within her body.

Initiation

A rite of passage from one state of being to another. It can be a religious or spiritual act such as baptism, or induction into a coven, group, or tradition; a tribal or cultural rite such as coming into womanhood, graduation, marriage, and so on; a natural phase or event such as puberty, first sexual experience, or the death of someone close. Initiation permanently alters the consciousness of the participant, opening new doors of experience.

Invoke

To call a force or deity into oneself, another person, or ritual space, often by means of spoken words or invocation.

Isis

Egyptian goddess who stems from Inanna/Ishtar, and on whom the Virgin Mary's symbolism is based. She is another manifestation of the Great Mother, a goddess of nature and the grain, whose lover, Osiris, is a dying and resurrecting vegetation god. She is Queen of the Heavens and Queen of Nature—roles that find a counterpart in the Priestess and Empress cards in tarot.

Jack in the Green

A manifestation of the Green Man, usually seen during traditional May Morning revelry, and usually acted by someone concealed within a leaf-covered wire frame.

Karma

Law of cause and effect. Whatever you do, for good or bad, is ultimately your responsibility, and the energy triggered by the act will come back to you eventually. This has to do with universal harmony and balance and has nothing to do with punishment (though it can feel like it sometimes).

The Lady

The Lady is the general term used to refer to the Goddess, particularly within traditional coven Wicca. It is the Goddess rather than any individual deity, but can also mean the Goddess as a force of Nature.

Lammas

One of the eight seasonal festivals. The first harvest. Grain harvest. Sacrifice of the God and John Barleycorn. August 1.

The Lord

Usually meaning the Horned God of Europe, but can mean the God as a single force rather than any individual manifestation of him.

Lord of the Greenwood

The ancient Horned God or Stag King of Europe.

Lugh

Celtic god of light, originating in Ireland.

Lughnasadh

The time of Lugh, when the first harvest was cut (Lammas). In Celtic times, this was also the season for marriages and contracts.

Mabon

The Celtic Child of Promise, who was stolen away when he was a baby and taken to the underworld, but later found and returned to his birthright. He is often portrayed playing a harp.

Maiden

Youthful phase of the Goddess, symbolised by the new moon.

Maiden of Flowers

Spring and early summer aspect of the goddess.

Mantra

A sacred sound or chant that is used to focus spiritual intent, especially during meditation.

Mercury

The Roman messenger god. His Greek counterpart was Hermes. Also the astrological planet of thought and communication.

Morris Dancers

Folk dancers with a tradition going back into the British pagan past. They dance, particularly at Beltane, with swords, bells, and handkerchiefs, and are clothed in white, with flower-covered hats on their heads.

Mother

Fruitful phase of the Goddess, symbolised by the full moon.

Norse

Coming from Norway originally. Now often used to denote some of the Northern Traditions that follow gods and goddesses of the Nordic pantheon, such as Freya, Odin, and Loki.

Oak King

Ancient summer aspect of the God.

Oestara/Spring Equinox

One of the eight seasonal festivals. The time of rebirth in early spring. Equal day and night with the days about to increase in length. March 21.

Oracle

In ancient times, the psychic seer who spoke out at a site dedicated to prophecy. These days, it can mean a form of divination such as tarot cards or runes.

Pathworking

A guided meditation using a tarot card or a path on the Tree of Life as a basis for visualisation.

Pentacle

A disk bearing a pentagram and, possibly, other symbols. Food, materials for spells, and other things can be placed on it on the altar. It belongs to earth.

Pentagram

Five-pointed star. The pentagram has been adopted as the symbol for witchcraft and paganism. The points represent the four elements and spirit.

Pomegranate

A round fruit in a bitter outer skin, with woody seeds inside encased in sweet, pink flesh. Particularly in Greek mythology, pomegranate seeds symbolise the mystical or the divine, and may represent a knowledge that changes those who taste them. Persephone was tricked into staying with Hades in the underworld by eating pomegranate seeds.

Prana

The life force that is present all around us, on which we can concentrate for magical work, or increase in our own systems by breathing exercises, meditation, yoga, exercise, correct diet, and so forth.

Qaballah/Kabala

Hebrew system of categorising the levels of being, spirituality, and so on. Sometimes called the Tree of Life.

Runes

A Norse and Anglo-Saxon script that is used for divination. The letters of the runic alphabet are inscribed on stones and cast in a reading, the juxtaposition and pattern of the individual letters having specific meanings.

Sacred Marriage

The Greenwood Marriage or mating of Goddess and God at Beltane. It is also the name for the union of male and female energies within Wicca, where it is undertaken between priest and priestess either as an act of sexual intercourse (usually in private, between lovers), or by lowering the athame into the chalice to bless the contents at the end of a rite or at one of the eight festivals.

Salamander

Personified symbol for the elemental forces of fire.

Samhain

Halloween. The Feast of the Dead. The Celtic New Year. Time when the veil between the worlds is thin and we can commune with the ancestors. October 31 to November 1.

Scrying

A method of divination that uses a reflective surface such as a mirror, bowl of water or crystal ball, smoke, and so on, to defocus the mind to assist clairvoyance.

Skyclad

A Wiccan term meaning unclothed (wearing only the sky). Many (but by no means all) witches work ritual this way.

Smudging

Wafting incense or herbal smoke over people, objects, or ritual space to cleanse them. Often used by practitioners of the Native American paths.

Solar

Of the sun.

Solitary

A witch who works alone, by choice or because of the difficulty of finding a coven.

Summer Solstice

One of the eight seasonal festivals. Midsummer festival of the sun's maximum power. Occurs around June 21.

Sylph

Personified symbol for the elemental forces of air.

Tarot

A system of divination of unknown origin, comprising seventy-eight cards that represent the many aspects of life.

Undine

Personified symbol for the elemental forces of water.

Wand

A short stave of wood used to direct energy in spell crafting. Can be used instead of the athame to cast the circle. It is ruled by fire.

Wheel of the Year

The round of eight festivals and the seasonal cycle.

Wiccan

Initiatory witchcraft, including Gardnerian and Alexandrian Wicca.

Yule/Winter Solstice

The sun's rebirth. One of the eight seasonal festivals. Occurs around December 21.

Index

☾ REACH FOR THE MOON

Llewellyn publishes hundreds of books on your favorite subjects! To get these exciting books, check your local bookstore or order them directly from Llewellyn.

Order by Phone
- Call toll-free within the U.S. and Canada, 1-800-THE MOON
- In Minnesota, call (651) 291-1970
- We accept VISA, MasterCard, and American Express

Order by Mail
- Send the full price of your order (MN residents add 7% sales tax) in U.S. funds, plus postage & handling to:
  Llewellyn Worldwide
  P.O. Box 64383, Dept. 0-7387-0172-6
  St. Paul, MN 55164–0383, U.S.A.

Postage & Handling
- Standard (U.S., Mexico, & Canada)

If your order is:
  $20.00 or under, add $5.00
  $20.01–$100.00, add $6.00
  Over $100, shipping is free
(Continental U.S. orders ship UPS. AK, HI, PR, & P.O. Boxes ship USPS 1st class. Mex. & Can. ship PMB.)
- Second Day Air (Continental U.S. only): $10.00 for one book + $1.00 per each additional book
- Express (AK, HI, & PR only) [Not available for P.O. Box delivery. For street address delivery only.]: $15.00 for one book + $1.00 per each additional book
- International Surface Mail: Add $1.00 per item
- International Airmail: Books—Add the retail price of each item; Non-book items—Add $5.00 per item

Please allow 4–6 weeks for delivery on all orders.
Postage and handling rates subject to change.

Discounts
We offer a 20% discount to group leaders or agents. You must order a minimum of 5 copies of the same book to get our special quantity price.

Free Catalog
Get a free copy of our color catalog, *New Worlds of Mind and Spirit*. Subscribe for just $10.00 in the United States and Canada ($30.00 overseas, airmail).

Visit our website at www.llewellyn.com for more information.